100+ Tactics for Office Politics

Second Edition

Casey Hawley, M.A.

BARRON'S

Dedication

To my family who gave me the passion for my work and the principles by which I live. These assets have undergirded my career and allowed me to hear that voice that tells one whether to go to the left or right in tricky situations.

Thriving in all sorts of office politics in diverse corporations has been less a matter of brilliance and more a matter of the discipline they gave me and the faith they shared with me.

Thank you Mom, Dad, Bobbi, and Jan.

All inquiries should be addressed to:
Barron's Educational Series, Inc.
250 Wireless Boulevard
Hauppauge, New York 11788
www.barronseduc.com

Library of Congress Catalog Card Number 2008000151

ISBN-13: 978-0-7641-3913-0
ISBN-10: 0-7641-3913-4

Library of Congress Cataloging-in-Publication Data

Hawley, Casey Fitts.
    100+ tactics for office politics / Casey Hawley. — 2nd ed.
        p.   cm. — (Business success guide)
    Includes index.
    ISBN-13: 978-0-7641-3913-0
    ISBN-10: 0-7641-3913-4
    1. Office politics. 2. Organizational behavior. 3. Corporate culture. 4. Success in business. I. Title. II. Title: One hundred plus tactics for office politics.

    HF5386.5.H38   20018
    650.1'3—dc22   2008000151

PRINTED IN CHINA
9 8 7 6 5 4 3 2 1

Contents

◆

Introduction

The New Office Politics—A Strategy

◆

Office politics have changed. The management books of the eighties and nineties are already outdated. Why? Here are just a few of the factors changing the way today's professional should deal with corporate politics:

◆ **Influence of Generation X, Generation Y, and the Digital Generation.** Don't try the old Managing by Objective (MBO) with these employees or it will backfire.

◆ **E-commerce, e-mail, and other Internet influences.** Today's technology is separating the old culture employees from the more liberated, new, Internet-savvy employee. Younger employees are quite literally more "plugged in." Their information and techniques are largely better and faster. Learn to work with these folks effectively or become a dinosaur.

◆ **Fast rate of change.** Mergers, going public, fierce competition, and a million other forces are making today's corporations change everything constantly. Change with it or kiss your career good-bye. Companies used to look for strategies that were long-term investments. Now, most look for what's the best move for this quarter. You must change your strategies, too.

◆ **Globalization.** Even small companies can do business all over the world thanks to the Internet. Learn to deal effectively with all kinds of cultures, values, and people.

PLAY TO WIN: OFFICE POLITICS

If you have decided to acknowledge that office politics really do exist and really do affect your pay, promotions, and working conditions, then you have taken the first step in mastering these politics. Office politics is a game that you *must* win. If you don't form a winning strategy, then you turn your career fate—success or failure—over to other people.

This book helps you take charge of your corporate destiny. By clearly defining your political options and offering strategies, the book enables you to make the smart moves.

In short, today's office politics require more flexibility and openness on your part. Handling tricky political situations also requires you to use your good judgment about what moves to make. Situations that crop up are dynamic and require you to make informed decisions based on the best information available, the people involved, and the risks and rewards to you.

This book gives you the inside information you need. Use your judgment to form a strategy for propelling your career forward. There are hundreds of powerful moves suggested here. To decide which are right for you, you must first assess the following points.

◆ How aggressive do you want to be?

◆ What kind of corporate culture are you in? Conservative? Start-up? Competitive?

◆ What fits with your personality?

◆ What will your values and ethics allow you to do comfortably?

◆ Which people will be affected by the move(s) you make? What are the risks? Rewards?

Empowered by this book, you can map out a clear and successful path to success in today's complex corporate world. Your good judgment will enable you to choose the right moves for you. Use the information in the following chapters to help you

◆ make the right moves.

◆ avoid false steps and costly mistakes.

◆ understand timing and what to do when.

◆ build up a network of supporters who will help you win successively better positions.

BONUS: ACTION ITEMS

Boost your success by completing the Action Item pages at the end of each chapter. These pages create a focused, fast-moving plan for your success. Implementing the Action Items brings you success sooner rather than later. Don't skip this life-changing page.

ABOUT THE AUTHOR

Casey Hawley has been a sought-after management consultant to Fortune 100 companies for almost 25 years. She has written their business plans, corporate communications strategies, and marketing materials. In doing so, she has learned in detail about every department and the dynamics within. She knows the visions of the people at the top as well as the issues of the people who make the organization work each day. Casey is the confidante to a wide range of executives and has her fingers on the pulses of companies that vary from the world's largest utilities to start-ups. If you want straightforward answers and strategies from an accomplished businessperson's perspective, *100+ Tactics for Office Politics* is the book for you.

In addition, Casey Hawley is the author of *100+ Winning Answers to the Toughest Interview Questions*, *How to Turn Any Employee Into a Star Performer*, *Loving and Living with Your Diabetic Spouse*, and *Effective Letters for Every Occasion*. Her web site, designed to help improve language for professionals, is *www. grammarcoach.com*. She also conducts three top-rated seminars nationally, *Powerful Business Writing*, *Proposal Workshop*, and *Career Change Management*.

Chapter 1

The 25 Critical Moves Every Professional Must Make

Do the right thing.

—Spike Lee

1. Always keep a professionally prepared, updated résumé ready to send out at a moment's notice.

The best career moves inside or outside your company often come out of nowhere. Don't miss your window of opportunity by delaying to prepare your résumé.

2. Learn to converse in a second language.

The workplace is becoming more multicultural. Corporations are now global in outlook. Knowing a second language makes you more versatile, useful, and promotable. Executives will also see your pursuit of a second language as a sign that you are sophisticated, aware of the changing marketplace, and headed up the corporate ladder. Doing this with other coworkers gives you an opportunity to practice your language skills. You may even be able to hire a high school foreign language teacher to tutor you as a group after hours at the office.

3. Know how to use the most current technology.

Have you considered using a smartphone, a PDA, or an LCD projection to make you more effective in your job? Do you know how to scan, download, and amend files easily?

And even if you are an executive and someone else retrieves your e-mail, you should *know how* to retrieve your e-mail yourself. Technology creeps into our conversation. You may find yourself looking like a dinosaur if you don't at least know how to use the latest technologies.

Many management careers went down the tubes during the down-sizings in the early nineties. Sometimes, deciding which of two managers to keep was very difficult for senior management. Even though computer skills were not really an important part of a senior manager's daily job, time and time again, lack of computer skills was the deciding factor in axing one individual and not the other. The interesting thing was that the reason for the firing was not that the computer skills were needed, but that the manager had shown no initiative in updating his skills.

Technology is an area that becomes outdated quickly. You can quickly expose your outdated ideas and skills if you don't familiarize yourself with the currently used technology in these areas.

◆ telecommunications
◆ information systems
◆ your industry technology

Some technologies are demonstrated in electronics stores. Vendors will come to your place of business to do demos for you. The Internet, magazines, and your local library are other excellent sources of information on technology.

4. Subscribe to an abstract service.

These services read the latest business books for you and give you an abridged version. No one today has time to read all the great business books out there. These synopsis services save you the time but deliver all the great ideas and content. Some, like *getAbstract.com*, are even online.

The executive level has an expectation that you are well read and current with the latest ideas in business circles. In upper-level conversations, you often hear, "Have you read . . . ?" Be prepared to

answer "Yes" by reading at least condensed versions of the good books out there.

5. Keep your friends close, your enemies closer.

This old saying is especially true in corporate America. I call it making friends with your dragons.

When I worked for a large management consulting firm, we were taught to identify our adversaries, whom our management called our "dragons," as quickly as possible. Because our firm sometimes recommended downsizing, you might think getting rid of these adversaries was our goal. Quite the contrary.

If an employee vocally or behaviorally rebelled at and was critical of everything our firm did, we viewed that person as a valuable asset. You see, your enemies will help you pinpoint weaknesses and flaws in your plans, projects, and thinking. Your adversaries will be honest with you about what you're doing wrong. They will usually give you far more valuable advice to help you avoid a failure than your friends will.

After identifying our enemies, our firm surprised them by asking them to serve on important decision-making committees and focus groups. We involved them in high-level meetings to help us make strategic decisions. We were honest with them about why we sought their cooperation. We acknowledged that they were doubtful of our ability to succeed and that they were critical of our methods. We told them that we needed insiders who saw things from that perspective because they might be right. We opened ourselves up to their criticism.

The "dragon" or adversarial employee transformed quickly from an agent who could make us fail to an internal consultant with a vested interest in our success. Several great results came from making friends with our dragon.

◆ The dragon offered criticism constructively to us rather than destructively disseminating his criticism behind our backs.
◆ The dragon saw the mistakes we were about to make and often told us how to avoid them.
◆ Fighting against the dragon would have made his attack on us more ferocious and destructive. Going to the dragon and petitioning his help collapsed the dynamic of "him versus us." We took away the element of conflict.
◆ The dragon was flattered by the respect we gave to his opinions. Often, highly negative, critical employees are bitter because they have not received the respect, attention, or status they feel they are due. It's very heady stuff to have an outsider say, "You have some valuable insights that are beyond what we have. Can you share your expertise, knowledge of this corporate culture, and insight? Will you help us?"

◆ Other employees were dramatically impressed when the famous dragon chose to become a part of our team. Having the dragon on a committee or even leading a focus group said to others:
- There's something of value that the management firm is doing or the dragon wouldn't invest his time.
- The things the dragon feared are the things we feared. If the dragon feels comfortable with the initiatives taken by this company, then I can feel comfortable participating, too.
- This company really wants to look at all sides of an issue. They're not just steamrolling through, forcing this project on us. They are genuinely seeking input from all employees, all management.

In a short time, the dragon would become our most devoted supporter. Our services and strategies were good ones, designed to improve the financial viability of the company and preserve jobs. Once the dragon stopped roaring long enough to hear our plans, he became part of the positive momentum toward success.

6. Hang out with the best people.

To do this, follow these guidelines:

◆ Accept every invitation possible if issued by people a level higher than you are in the company. Who cares if they're boring? They need to get to know you if they're going to help advance your career. Besides, even if you don't care for them, some of their peers may be invited.
◆ Befriend people at your level who are most likely to move up the corporate ladder. You will have more in common with them as time goes on, even if right now they appear to be very different. This will also increase your exposure to their power base, which can help you advance.
◆ Reciprocate invitations and entertaining. Don't be stingy.

7. **Plant constant positive messages about your work and your department.**

To succeed, become a one-person PR machine. It's not the people who quietly go about producing the most work or the highest-quality work that get the promotions. The people who are rewarded are the ones who can impress most by hyping what they do. Of course, the best approach is to turn out high-quality work in quantity *and* hype it. Still, we all know people who don't seem that talented or productive but always seem to be perceived as stars. How does one do that?

One strategy is to conduct good news campaigns. The good news campaign puts one of the most powerful tools in your organization to work for you: the grapevine. Oh, I know you have been told how unreliable the grapevine is. Not true. According to most surveys, the grapevine is 80 to 90 percent accurate. Plus, people tend to believe what they hear through the grapevine. After all, don't many of the rumors you hear through your corporate grapevine turn out to be true?

HOW TO CONDUCT A GOOD NEWS CAMPAIGN

Whenever you begin a new project or task, look for anything valuable, profitable, or interesting in what you are doing. Then pointedly drop those facts into conversations with everyone you meet, whether they are in a high or low position. Examples:

◆ If you are writing your company's business plan, say:

Writing this business plan has yielded some surprising results. We found that our department handled 15 percent more cases last year without any increase in staff.

or

Yes, the business plan has turned out very nicely. We're all pleased.

♦ If you are in sales, look for profit increases, volume increases, and improved customer satisfaction, as well as increases in number of sales. Say:

We've even surprised ourselves at how we've been able to improve our profit margin on sales.

♦ If you are in an administrative or operations role, say:

Our efforts to streamline the payroll process have really paid off.

or

It took some time to analyze how to improve product delivery but the results have been great.

So when exactly do you say these things? Constantly; for example:

♦ waiting for an elevator. People will eavesdrop and carry this positive gossip to other departments.

♦ in those minutes just before a meeting starts while people are making small talk. Make small talk work for you

♦ in the copy room

♦ in the breakroom

♦ in focus groups or committee meetings

♦ at lunch

8. Conduct your career path with savvy by taking these critical steps.

♦ Always know the salaries of your coworkers, competitors, and others who do jobs similar to yours. Know what you're worth.

♦ Make a habit of communicating your goals of advancing to your boss and others. Don't hesitate to negotiate for raises and promotions. Set the expectation that you expect to advance. Prepare an intelligent and well-documented case for yourself as you lobby for more money or status. Remember these sayings:

The squeaky wheel gets the grease.

The more you ask the more you get.

◆ Don't be afraid to ask your boss to reconsider your evaluation or your application for promotion. If initially he says "No" to a promotion, ask what you can do to earn a "Yes" next time. Then ask your boss to revisit this with you within a set time, say three or six months.

◆ Be willing to move.

◆ Document everything you do: every accomplishment, every service you provide, every committee, things promised you, any improvements, any new training, civic contributions, etc.

9. Have a panic plan.

This is a well-prepared plan for how you will respond when something negative occurs. No matter how successful you are, there will be small or large setbacks along the way. You must master the following responses so that you will be seen as a model of grace under pressure, cool professionalism, and unparalleled competence. You can actually gain a lot of support and admiration by the way others perceive your handling of a disaster. Here's how:

◆ Have a stash of noncommittal phrases. These will help you respond to someone without really committing yourself. Sometimes, a crisis is dumped in our laps by a person who is emotional and demanding an answer. Until you have had time to think the situation through, you don't want to toss off an answer you may regret.

One technique is to agree with part of what the other person says.

– If your boss says, "You're not showing any results in improving quality control in the Southwest Region. I've just seen the figures. Rework has increased by 10 percent. We will never meet our performance pay goals at this rate. In fact, we'll both be lucky if we keep our jobs."

You say, "A 10 percent increase in rework is not acceptable. I know improving our southwestern locations is a key part of your strategic plan for improving production. It is urgent that I look into this and get all the answers so I can reverse this. Can you give me until tomorrow to formulate a plan of attack?"

– If your biggest customer says, "Your shipment of corn syrup arrived so late that we had to halt production on one brand of our cereal. That cost me thousands of dollars. I'm pulling my account."

You say: "There is no good excuse for a valuable customer like you to be disappointed like this. I realize the cost in terms of production, lost time, and your personal inconvenience. I hope you will allow me to track down the source of the problem. It may be the shipper. If it is my company, we won't tolerate it—you're too important to us. We also have a better on-time delivery record than anyone in the industry. Our reputation is at stake here. Please allow me to fix it."

– What if a potential customer says, "I like your products but your prices are the highest in the industry?"

You say, "Well, there is the issue of cost—upfront and total long-term cost. Have you assessed the amount of time and effort you are spending straightening out problems with your present vendor? We have. Let me show you how these costs are offset by a number of things."

The responses above may seem painfully obvious, but in a fast exchange of words they have a positive effect.

◆ If you are being fired, ask for the moon. That's right. Most people are caught off guard and are humiliated, so they feel they can't ask for much—or they're so stunned they forget to ask. The day you are fired, you should calmly and in an informed way set some expectations,
   – what insurance benefits you will need from your company and how long you expect to receive them
   – other benefits, temporary use of a vehicle, etc.
   – use of an office and office services while you conduct a job search
   – services of a career counselor or placement service
   – any paid leave due you
   – bonuses or commissions due in the future
   – an opportunity to work for your company as a contractor or part-time employee

◆ You should have a decision-making grid. Develop a simple grid system that forces you to be logical and analyze problems objectively even when you're very upset. Example:
  – Look at a choice you are about to make. List answers to these questions:
    What are the worst consequences if I do this?
    How likely are they to occur?
    What positive results could happen?
    How likely are they?
◆ Before a problem ever occurs, establish a list of three people whose judgment you trust and who know you well. In a crisis, submit the list above. Ask what they think you should do.
◆ Listen to your instincts. Instincts often alert us early to problems.

10. Develop a repertoire of appropriate nonverbal responses.

Learn to put on your "game face." Every major corporation that has ever done a survey on communication has found that what we say is not nearly as important as how we look when we say it. Usually, nonverbal communication rates as 80 to 93 percent of our effectiveness. Nonverbal communication includes facial expressions, posture, stance, gestures, and things people see.

11. Learn to play like the big boys.

If golf is the sport of the level above you, start lessons today. If racquetball is the passion, join the club that attracts the leaders in your company. This opportunity for exposure and networking is worth more than a thousand hours of overtime.

12. Master meetings.

Meetings focus attention on you in a way no other job activity does. To get anywhere, you must learn to be the perfect participant and to conduct meetings.

To be a perfect participant, master five skills.

◆ Ask great questions. This shows you're listening and your management will feel gratified. A good question also reveals your intelligence and business savvy.

◆ Prepare for meetings. If are attending a meeting on Wednesday, on Tuesday you should prepare for it even if you are not presenting. Review the agenda and the topics. Gather any information needed to help you ask intelligent questions. Bring any facts or figures with you that others may want.

◆ Predict who will attend the meeting. What was on John's mind the last time you met? Be sure to bring that up and ask for an update. Visualize each person. What is the right thing to say to each one?

◆ Keep an interested expression on your face at all times. Don't doodle, distract, look at the time, or exchange looks with others while the speaker is speaking.

◆ Take notes. That gratifies some people.

When you conduct a meeting follow these rules:

◆ Always hand out a simple agenda.
◆ Never go overtime.
◆ Don't call a meeting unless it's necessary.
◆ Prepare a dynamite opening and definite closing. Practice both to leave an impression of professionalism.

13. Learn to write the following before you need to:

◆ a business case
◆ a business plan
◆ a proposal
◆ a thank-you note
◆ a report

Some avenues of learning are

◆ seminars
◆ books
◆ documents written by successful people in your company

14. Embrace change.

Executives are used to a lot of grumbling about change. Change is inevitable so set yourself apart from others by expressing enthusiasm.

◆ Accept moves, if at all possible. Most CEOs have been willing to relocate.
◆ Don't lock in one image of yourself and block out other possibilities. The most successful marketing people I know are technical or operations people who never thought they were the marketing type. Because they chanced a change—or were forced to—their incomes zoomed.

◆ Be the first to welcome and offer your help to new people, particularly those above you. They never forget the first people who warmed to them.

15. Your most valuable investment of time will be in people.

◆ Network (see Chapter 6).
◆ Mentor others. The people on their way up can help make or break your career. Among those will be a few stars who will one day be your peers or even your boss.
◆ Be the best listener in your company. Learn to make someone feel thoroughly listened to. Pause after the other person's last word before jumping in with your comment. That gives the appearance that you are thoroughly considering what he is saying. Maintain good eye contact. Follow up a day or two later. Mention something specific that he said. This does more for your image than a library of opinions or facts.
◆ Support and encourage others; they will usually support and encourage you.
◆ Attend company or departmental social gatherings. Entertain appropriately.

16. Congratulate, acknowledge, and thank.

Do this face to face but also put it in writing. Follow-up notes are a hallmark of a person on the way up.

◆ Congratulate people on anything: successfully finishing a difficult project, being appointed to an influential committee, joining a civic organization, plus the usual promotions.
◆ Acknowledge people for their contributions, their team rather than selfish motivations, input, their consistent performance, a reference to them in your city or company newspaper.

◆ Thank people for everything: inviting you to a meeting, planning a seminar, taking time out to help you, any small gift, and so on.

Become a note writer. Make sending out a quick note part of your daily routine.

17. Be a lifelong learner.

Keep current on all things new in business and culture. Don't allow your thinking to become outdated. Here's how:

◆ Read current magazines and newspapers. To me, the *Wall Street Journal* is still tops.
◆ Read three best-selling nonfiction books a year and discuss them with others. Business and leadership books are preferred.
◆ Invest in tutors and consultants. Often a tutor can teach you precisely what you need to know most urgently about a software package, a foreign language, or a new undertaking. Although the per hour cost is high, you will use your time and resources much more effectively.
◆ Attend training, seminars, and conferences.

18. Ask your boss for a development plan.

A development plan is a plan that outlines the things you need to do to develop into a more valuable employee, be promotable to the next level, and succeed in your organization. Development plans are valuable for these reasons:

◆ You gain a more accurate view of what your company values and wants from you. Employees often invest a lot of time and energy in tasks that the company will never reward. We have a myopic perspective. The development plan helps you see it *their* way and *they* have the power.

◆ A development plan is win/win. You become more valuable to the company.
◆ Asking for a development plan demonstrates your willingness to change, be flexible, learn new things, and take constructive criticism. Executives value those things. When you embark on a development plan, you may win fans for simply opening yourself up to *trying* to make the effort.
◆ A development plan is excellent documentation in case you are ever passed over unfairly for promotion.

Caution: Development plans may also be used to document weaknesses as a basis for termination. Beware of taking this step if you are vulnerable or if your boss is not supportive of you.

19. Learn positive negotiation skills.

Get interactive training with role plays. You don't need theory; you need to know how to do this vital part of winning at work. What type of things do you need to learn to negotiate?

◆ Deadlines
◆ Larger portions of the budget
◆ Salary increases
◆ Personnel. (Ask for another person to split a territory or a temp to reduce that mountain of paperwork.)
◆ Better severance package
◆ Flexible maternity leave

20. Do the dirty work.

The following are examples of ways to apply this to practice.

◆ No one ever wants to be in charge of the business plan. Volunteer, especially if it looks like you'll be assigned it anyway. Then delegate. In fact, accept the assignment with the contingency that others will help. Assign each person a small part. Hire a consultant to clean up the final draft. Take full credit.

◆ Volunteer to make all the food arrangements for the department picnic. You will look like a generous host using company money. You'll work very hard for a few days, but you'll get lots of recognition. You've worked very hard before, but with no recognition. How about getting something out of it?

◆ Choose a holiday and work it every year. A few people I know love working between Christmas and New Year's. They say that no one is there, and they get lots done. Also, the pace is slower, more laid back. So many people take off at this time that covering responsibilities is a problem for management. Sacrifice. You may find it enjoyable.

21. Volunteer to help coworkers in a time crunch.

This makes people owe you big time.

The most powerful application of this step is to help others in a crisis.

◆ Observe when coworkers are working on large projects with deadlines.
◆ The last week of their project, plan a light schedule for yourself.
◆ Volunteer to stay late to input data, put together handouts, help coworker practice a presentation, do any menial job.

This last-minute gift of your time will never be forgotten.

22. Know corporate and social etiquette and exhibit impeccable manners.

Take courses. Read books. Ask others for help.

23. Learn the many techniques for resolving conflict.

One or two conflicts along the way can alter your career destiny. Everyone will have conflicts—large and small. How you solve conflict and *initially respond* to conflict is what advances your career or damages it. Learning to express empathy for the other person's position, offering attractive compromises, controlling your physical response (blushing, raising your voice, nervousness), and many other skills can help you come out of a conflict stronger than you were before. Sometimes a conflict is the beginning of great communication with a coworker and even the beginning of a friendship. Learn to attack problems but lift up people.

24. Promote diversity.

Ours is truly a global economy. Learn to work with respect, support, and joy with all people. Abandon any prejudices based on gender, race, religion, or nationality.

25. Have a clear understanding of your values.

Know what your spiritual and ethical beliefs are. Write them down. Don't violate these or you will become ineffective.

If you have difficulty defining your values, try this exercise. Ask yourself what you would do if you had only one week to live. That's a good starting point to define what you value. You should also resolve what you believe about

◆ God and religion
◆ marriage, family, and children
◆ accumulation of wealth
◆ success
◆ charity and giving to the community
◆ retirement
◆ death
◆ material possessions and which ones are most important to you
◆ who your best friends are

ACTION ITEMS

1. List the top three items on the list of 25 moves that you think will do your career the most good.

_____

_____

_____

2. Choose the most important move above to further your career.

3. Today, do something specific to help you make this move. For example, if your most important move is number 3—knowing how to use the most current technology—you could take one of the concrete steps below.

   ◆ Sign up for a course on how to use the Internet more effectively.
   ◆ Trade in your cell phone for one that offers wireless e-mail and learn to use it.
   ◆ Read an article on the latest PDA devices. Decide which model, if any, is right for your needs.

4. Do one more specific activity that will help you make progress toward the critical move listed above.

5. Repeat Step 3 for another move.

Chapter 2

The 25 Career
Blowers to Avoid

Show me a person who has never made a mistake and I'll show you somebody who has never achieved much.

—Joan Collins

Every organization has a few people who at one time were viewed as most likely to succeed but never did. People make comments like the following about these bright, accomplished failures.

◆ Everyone thought she might be the first female CEO of our company, but she blew it.
◆ I don't know what happened to him. In his early career, he could do no wrong.
◆ He was climbing up the ladder quickly—one promotion after another, but he crossed the wrong person. They'll never let him in at the top now.

◆ When he was younger, he was the golden boy around here. For some reason, he just topped off at this level.

◆ She's really smart and her department exceeds productivity goals every quarter. I wonder why she hasn't been promoted?

The opportunities to self-sabotage a career are many. This chapter examines the top 25 wrong moves to make. These false steps, career derailing detours, and blunders have stunted more careers than any others.

The first eight are listed as pairs. In many cases a career mistake is caused by a lack of balance. For example, look at the first two career blowers. Number one is "Not having a plan for your career." Number two is "Being unwilling to depart from your plan." Either one of those indicates a lack of balance in one direction or the other. Seeking balance in this case and in many of the others is what is called for in order to achieve success.

1. Not having a plan for your career.

What do you do when you want to reach a destination that you've never reached before? You get a map. You plot your moves and turns. You ask for advice from others who have made the journey before you.

Reaching a career goal is just the same. You waste years if you wander aimlessly and hope success "just happens." Yes, that happens to a few lucky folks. So does winning the lottery. The difference is that in career success, you can fix the odds by developing and planning the steps you will take to arrive at the pinnacle of your career.

How do you create a plan for your success?

- ◆ What is your ultimate goal? List that.
- ◆ What are the educational and training requirements you will need?
- ◆ What job experience will you need? How can you begin to get that experience?
- ◆ Ask your mentor and other seasoned professionals to look at your plan. Ask them to tell you things you need to do to reach your goal. You should also contact a professional recruiter who hires people for the type of job you are seeking. Ask her to tell you the skills and training she looks for when placing someone in these jobs. If you have a boss who is unselfish and interested in helping you move up, ask for her help, too.
- ◆ Design an action plan for accomplishing all you need to do to reach your goal. An example is included as the last chapter of this book. Set one- and five-year goals.

2. **Being unwilling to depart from a career plan.**

Many things can happen that make changing your original plan a good idea. Still, old-fashioned thinking sometimes causes people to refuse to back away from an original plan. Changing a career plan is inevitable in today's ever-changing work environment. Here are just a few of the valid reasons to depart from your plan.

- ◆ *A new and valuable opportunity arises that takes you in a different direction.* Scott Johnson was on the rise as a political consultant and analyst. He assisted Newt Gingrich until the latter's surprising resignation in 1999. Because events moved quickly leading up to the former Speaker's abrupt announcement of resignation, Scott found himself without a job for the first time in his impressive career. While he was biding his time awaiting the inevitable job offers, he decided to pursue photography as a hobby, something he had always wanted to learn. As it turned out, Scott had an immense, undiscovered talent for photography. He did some shots for our local Chamber of Commerce and the rest is history: Scott is one of the most talented young commercial photographers in the United States today. Not only that, but he has a passion for photography that makes each workday exhilarating for him.

◆ *You gain some experience in the field you're pursuing and find it's not what you thought it would be.* Some careers look more attractive to observers than they actually are. Many people attracted to investment careers think they want to be stockbrokers. Novice brokers quickly learn they are just salesmen and that the investment analysis is left to others in their firms. The turnover rate among stockbrokers, sales managers, medical students, teachers, and other professions is high. After taking everything into consideration, decide whether you need to amend your career plan.

◆ *Technology changes, the job market changes, anything changes.* You find that your career plan is outdated and not as conducive to success as it once was.

3. Being obviously controlling.

Wanting to be in control of your future, your worklife, and, to some degree, your coworkers, is normal. When you become too controlling, however, bad things happen to your career.

◆ People rebel and resist doing anything you want.
◆ You will be viewed as a manipulator. If you are reading this book, you have already shown a desire to do whatever is in your control to help yourself. Displaying your quest to con-

trol your destiny will not be popular. People will see you as manipulative.

You must learn to manipulate without appearing manipulative. Learn to control situations subtly through influencing, not aggression. Backdoor moves or other unattractive behaviors can sabotage your career. Read Chapters 3 and 9 to learn how to get people to support you in a positive way.

◆ Your political enemies will have ammunition against you. Even if the moves you're making are in the company's best interests, you may appear selfish.
◆ You can appear ridiculous.
◆ High control behavior over a long period of time inevitably leads to burnout. It just takes too much energy to juggle so much for so long.

4. **Being too passive.**

Wishy-washy behavior does not command respect. Being a take-charge person still inspires confidence if done the right way. Although there are times to be noncommittal, in most daily situations coworkers and management admire straight answers, strong decision making, and clear responses to questions. The people on the fast track take the initiative. Those who take the road of passivity because they think it's safe may find they have no place in a dynamic, viable organization.

5. **Being unwilling to take a risk.**

If you interview most CEOs and ask what pivotal moves got them where they are today, they will usually cite a risk or two. To gain the attention of people at the top, you need to develop the discernment to evaluate risks. Learn to assess quickly which risks are worth taking. Leadership belongs to the risk takers, not the protectors of the status quo.

> One of the key reasons to take risks is to avoid appearing outdated. Not taking risks or refusing to try new things quickly outdates even brilliant professionals. Our business practices and thinking can age quickly in today's society.

Attend conferences. Read current news and industry and cultural articles.

6. **Taking uncalculated risks.**

Consideration should go into each risk we take because there is a downside. That's why we call it a risk. Jumping at an opportunity without considering the impact to others and ourselves can create enemies for us. Think it out.

A client of mine, Thomas, worked for a large telecommunications company. A vendor calling on him shared an idea for a new service that would help reduce the monthly bill for virtually every residential customer. Thomas resigned from his upper-management position abruptly to become a partner with his vendor. Thomas felt this idea was going to be a winner, and he wanted to be in on the ground floor.

If Thomas had taken the time to do a competitive study, he would have realized how many other people were bringing almost identical services to the market. Thomas' new company failed. He was fortunate that his old company took him back; however, he is working several levels below his last position.

7. **Not making allies of the little people.**

If your goal is to be a big shot, you may underestimate how effectively the little people you run into along the way can bring you down. The same way the Lilliputians tied down Gulliver, seemingly unpowerful people can block you and hamstring your career. Secretaries, nonmanaging professionals, coworkers, and even hourly workers may be influencers on more powerful people. And be sure to play nice with the reception staff and mail room employees; these gatekeepers can facilitate your communication or damage it.

8. **Investing too much time in the little people.**

You can befriend everyone at work but you can't be everyone's best friend. Don't make it a habit to get into regular, lengthy conversations with coworkers about the details of their lives; you look like you have time to waste.

9. **Becoming identified with only one project, one group, or one skill.**

Corporate winds are constantly shifting. What is viewed as popular and cutting edge today can turn out to be a very bad idea next month. If you become known for your work on only one project, you may find yourself out of the loop when your company abandons its interest in that project. How would you have liked to have been the company expert on eight-track tapes or the Edsel? The current project you're working on could be their equivalent!

What should you do to prevent becoming a one-hit wonder? Ask to work on at least one other project or product in your company. Serve on a focus group or as a consultant.

Let others see that you have more than one dimension to your skills. If your company shuts down the widget division, be sure it knows that you have the flexibility to do other things besides make widgets. When management lets all the widget employees go, you will have allies on other projects who will be able to scope out a place for you somewhere else.

Just as dangerous is to be identified with one clique or one faction in a company. The group may be the hot young guns, the tekkies, the enlightened leadership, the adventure/athletic crowd, the bean counters, or any other group that hangs together.

10. Using alcohol or prescripton drugs unwisely.

Sometimes, we are so flattered to be asked to join the boss for a drink that we don't think about the negative consequences. Your boss may offer you alcohol, but if you accept he may be a little disappointed in you, especially if it's at lunch. The boss may be thinking, "When I was in his position, I had too much work to do to be drinking at lunch," or "I can drink because I'm going back to the office, but clients may detect liquor on his breath this afternoon."

You should make it a policy to never drink in the daytime. Evening drinks are another matter. You may be in a culture that encourages alcohol consumption. You may choose to drink but drink moderately, or you may choose to abstain entirely. In today's mineral water society, many businesspeople have sworn off drinking for fitness or other reasons. Nondrinkers are accepted and often admired.

Prescription drugs are a growing problem in the workplace. The stresses that cause problems in our backs, necks, and psyches combined with the aging boomer population, have yielded a variety of problems that require medication. Helpful medications, if misused, can potentially cause career problems. These include

◆ muscle relaxers
◆ migraine medications
◆ pain medications
◆ antidepressants
◆ stimulants

11. Inappropriate conversation.

Do not participate in conversations that include the following:

◆ humor or comments that demean any race, nationality, gender, religion, or age group
◆ profanity or disregard for any religion, including using God's name in vain. (**Note:** Many people exclaim, "God," when they are excited or surprised. This is highly offensive to a large portion of the population and appears uncouth.)
◆ graphic conversations about digestive functions, illness, wounds, diseases, or surgeries. This is distasteful to many people.

12. **Being unwilling to move or go back to school or make some other sacrifice to advance your career.**

You send out a signal early on that says, "I'm expecting advancement and I'm willing to do what it takes to boost my career." If you aren't willing to go where the promotions are or get the degrees needed, you basically are saying, "What I have now is fine for me. I'm content where I am."

Gone are the days when the brightest people could become managers or even executives without degrees. Although young people often point to success stories like Bill Gates and Stephen Jobs who made it in the technology field without degrees, keep in mind that these are the exceptions. For every Bill Gates, you have a thousand computer programmers working midnight to 7 A.M. for $15 per hour. Get the degrees your field values. Education is almost always a great investment with a high return.

13. **Making poor first impressions.**

Think of how many times a great first impression can boost your career and your income:

◆ job interviews
◆ committees you served on with other departments
◆ meetings with clients, vendors, and others
◆ introductions to executives
◆ social events that provide networking opportunities

What can you do if you're not making a great first impression? First, find out specifically what you are doing wrong.

◆ Do you come off as arrogant?
◆ Do your nonverbals say you lack confidence?
◆ Is your voice too loud? Fast? Soft?

◆ How is your eye contact?

◆ Do you talk too little or too much?

◆ How is your appearance? Demeanor?

◆ Do you say positive or gracious things when introduced?

Ask your boss, your former boss, your coworkers, and anyone else to critique you. Get the training or resources you need to change. This one is important. Work on it.

14. Bringing your personal life into the workplace.

Although it is forbidden by law for our personal choices to affect our career path and income, the reality is that they do. Of course, the first advice is to leave all talk about your dates, your marriage, and your spouse outside the office. Still, people around us eventually learn about our lifestyle. Having dating habits that fly in the face of our corporate culture or marrying the "wrong" person can diminish us in the eyes of the people we need to impress.

You may think that if your work is good that you will not be judged by whom you choose to date or how you conduct your personal life. Wrong. People love to talk about these issues. If you are in a yuppie, status-conscious organization and you are dating Hulga, the biker barmaid, there will be talk. As unfair as it is, people will begin to doubt your good judgment in work-related areas. This should not be true, but it is.

And before you marry, be sure that your spouse shares the same vision of the future and your career as you do.

If conflict does arise, communicate fully at home. You don't want your spouse to feel compelled to call and discuss this while you are at work.

15. **Not actively putting out publicity on your accomplishments, projects, and contributions.**

Everything you do should be announced, written about, and accidentally on purpose brought up in conversation. This is not elementary school where nominating yourself for office is considered a breach of conduct. Blow your own horn—in a nice, professional way. Read the strategies in Chapter 6.

16. **Talking negatively. Every day you should communicate at least one positive thing about your department or yourself through a casual work conversation.**

Speak positively about others, too. People will perceive you as successful if you are usually the source of good news about yourself and others.

Ken Blanchard, author of *The One Minute Manager*, gives some great advice. He says to train yourself to "Catch people doing something right." He points out that even mediocre observers can see something that is out of whack. It takes an exceptional person to notice what someone has done correctly.

17. **Little thefts.**

Misuse of company funds in any way, direct or indirect, is never profitable. Even if you feel justified in overstating your expense report, don't do it. Even if you know that everyone brings pens and legal pads home for personal use, don't do it. The cost to your career could be much greater. You need only one boss who sees this as dishonesty to get a black mark on your career. Even if your boss says nothing to you about this, helping yourself to company property may diminish your credibility and you may not be trusted with greater things. Why risk a lot for so little?

18. Gossip.

Never gossip. Here are a few of the many reasons. Gossip is not a smart career move because it

◆ hurts your credibility
◆ makes enemies for you
◆ is not always true, so you may be viewed as a liar
◆ is often true and hurts people deeply
◆ gives the appearance you have nothing to do but waste time
◆ imbues you with the characteristics of malice and jealousy
◆ may entrap you in your own words

19. Manage time poorly.

Gossip is only one way of demonstrating to management that we have plenty of time to waste. Here are some other telltale signs that you are not responsible enough to manage your own time:

◆ being a familiar face in the breakroom, smoking area, or other hangouts
◆ making or receiving personal telephone calls
◆ spending company time on personal e-mails or surfing the Internet. Many companies have software monitoring how much time you waste on pursuits such as these. More embarrassing, they read the words and review the sites you thought were private.
◆ making elaborate preparations to do a task; spending as much time setting up as you spend performing
◆ taking long lunch hours or breaks
◆ arriving late, leaving early
◆ writing checks, doing charitable work, doing any personal

business on company time. This is a pet peeve of some people in your management.

◆ talking and visiting with coworkers too much
◆ procrastinating
◆ rushing through a job and doing sloppy work

20. Unprofessional image.

Your hair, grooming, and dress are only part of professional image. These factors are also important:

grammar
posture
smile
behavior

Here are some tips for improving your image as needed.

◆ If your grammar isn't perfect, ask a high school or junior college teacher to tutor you, perhaps twice a month.
◆ Smile often. Smile even before you answer the phone; you will have a friendlier tone. Most of us are difficult to read. A smile sends an immediate positive message and puts the other person at ease.

21. Making empty threats.

Before you ever make a threat or issue an ultimatum, make sure you are prepared to live with the consequences. Extremely valuable employees often feel they have more leverage than they do, but companies do stupid things all the time. Valuable employees lose their jobs; they are not immune.

22. Being obsessive-compulsive about projects, subjects, or tasks.

It's a good idea to push yourself and others to some degree to meet deadlines and achieve goals, but you can go too far and alienate your coworkers. You may even find yourself alienating your boss who set the deadline in the first place. In today's workplace, flexibility is often valued above rigid adherence to deadlines and specifications.

People who have no problems with burnout or organizational change are more willing to do the following:

- ask to amend project goals and deadlines
- compromise on minor things to achieve major things
- ask others for help
- ask for other resources
- admit when they have mistakenly underestimated a project
- resist the temptation to push and tell people what they must, ought, or should do

At one time, the maxim was, "Always meet a deadline or goal, no matter what you have to do." Although this is still a fine ideal, you may have unexpected occurrences that make this impossible in today's business culture of constant interruptions. Go to coworkers as a friend in need, not like Chicken Little saying that "the sky will fall" if this doesn't get done.

Younger employees, especially, don't like very intense or authoritative people. Ask to collaborate. Ask for a favor. People like to help an underdog; they resist pushers. You want to exit this project with your network of helpers stronger, not weaker, because of their efforts.

23. Neglecting community service.

The higher you go in the corporate strata, the more public service is expected from you. You will associate with more executives sooner in your career if you volunteer and serve as an officer in a civic organization or high-profile charity. Listed below are some great organizations that are good investments of your time.

◆ United Way
◆ Chamber of Commerce
◆ Any Kiwanis group that is popular with executives in your company. Find out the one they attend.
◆ Local popular conservation groups: Save the River, Clean up the Forest, and other organizations.
◆ Historic preservation groups: Save a Landmark, Preserve Downtown. Be careful not to choose a group that blocks progress that business needs.

As your name is seen in the papers, often linked with executive volunteers and contributors, people will begin to see you as part of that successful group. You will be amazed at how accepting these groups are of newcomers. A willing pair of hands is always needed.

Naturally, you should volunteer because it's the right thing to do. As you succeed, you should feel obligated to give back to the community. That's part of the reason you will find so many executives devoting time to these activities.

24. Making enemies and letting people down.

You may do long-term damage to your career by simply letting people down.

◆ You fail to do something you agreed to do.
◆ You don't go out on a limb and support someone who's criticized.
◆ Your contribution to a project is weak or poorly executed.
◆ You accept a job and must leave this person or team.
◆ You sell out in some way. You let them down by leaving the department for more money, or allying more with senior management, or doing something they believe is selling out.

On the other hand, sometimes we make outright enemies by

◆ being perceived as dishonest. Perhaps your view is that you changed your mind. Your enemy may not see it that way.
◆ making a move that costs another person money, resources, time, vacation days, or anything.
◆ being the new kid on the block. Sometimes, you haven't even had time to do anything and you're already highly resented.

◆ rivalry of equals. Sometimes, when someone is too much like you, a competitive relationship ignites. You can be similar in expertise or similar in intelligence or similar in background. Handled negatively, a rival can become a powerful, well-equipped enemy.

◆ unequal rivals. If your rival is out to prove she is just as talented, just as intelligent, or just as qualified as you, you may have a greater problem if she really isn't. Fierce competitors may have difficulty accepting that the better woman won a certain position or honor. Wannabes who are passed over can expend a tremendous amount of energy sabotaging and disparaging you. Read Chapter 1, Career Move Number 5, on befriending your dragons.

25. Abusing Internet or e-mail communication tools.

The Internet has provided many opportunities for saving time and improving the flow of information. It has also presented us with as many opportunities for wasting time and alienating those with whom we share information. Most companies today have software that reports to your management daily where you go online, how much time you spent, and what you said in your e-mail. If you use a company account or equipment, the company can view every word you send or receive. The day of "Big Brother" has arrived. Here are a few "don'ts" for Internet/e-mail users.

E-mail don'ts

◆ Copy and send e-mails to just everyone. People are annoyed at being on a cc list for everything. Be selective. Don't junk up someone else's mailbox with information not really needed.

◆ Phrase cute or obscure subject headings. Instead, state what your subject is so clearly that a busy person can tell at a glance what your topic will be. Many people today preview the subject lines only through a special filter on their e-mail system. They don't see your entire e-mail when they scan, only your subject line. Make it clear.

◆ Send attachments when you can copy text into the e-mail itself. Some people dislike having to open attachments. Their computers may take time switching from one program to another. If at all possible, copy and paste information from your attachment into the e-mail.

◆ Put in writing anything you don't want everyone in your organization to see. E-mail is the least private form of communication in your company. Remember that.

◆ Write carelessly and ungrammatically. E-mails have lives of their own. They get forwarded to people we did not intend them to go to. Busy people often forward e-mails to their bosses rather than retyping the information or making a phone call. We may have felt comfortable sending a sloppy e-mail to our original recipient, but she may have had the lack of judgment to pass it upward. E-mail is less formal, but it is not a license to write like a dunce.

E-mail do's

◆ Consider checking e-mails only at set times, once or twice a day. Constantly checking e-mails is a serious productivity problem; don't let it be yours. Some jobs require constant vigilance of e-mail, but most work better with a morning and late afternoon check.

◆ Ask your friends to send your personal e-mails to your home, not your office. All those jokes and stories take up a lot of memory when downloaded, not to mention taking up your time.

◆ Find out your company's rules regarding personal e-mails.

Internet don'ts

◆ Waste your employer's time surfing the Net. You would not bring in a hobby magazine, prop your feet up on your desk, and read leisurely. Don't abuse your time on the Internet.

◆ Use fee-based services for your personal use that are charged to your company.

◆ Go to inappropriate or unprofessional sites on your computer at work. Periodically, some companies check what sites have been visited by company computers. This could be embarrassing. Equally damaging is having someone walk by when you are on a site that is clearly not for business purposes.

ACTION ITEMS

List the five career blowers below that you think might be the greatest danger to your career. Be sure to list any that reflect a weakness that you know about.

1. Career Blower # _____

2. Career Blower # _____

3. Career Blower # _____

4. Career Blower # _____

5. Career Blower # _____

For each career blower, list a positive step you will take to avoid blowing it:

1. Career Blower # _____

2. Career Blower # _____

3. Career Blower # _____

4. Career Blower # _____

5. Career Blower # _____

Chapter 3

◆

How to Get Your Boss to Advance Your Career

Half our standards come from our first masters, and the other half from our first loves.

—George Santayana

HOW TO MANAGE YOUR BOSS

Joe Torre's Ground Rules for Success struck me as interesting from the moment I saw the table of contents. Torre devotes three chapters to dealing with bosses! Clearly, even a winner like Torre considers managing a boss a cornerstone of individual success.

Torre starts off with a rule every one of us can visualize. He says that when he starts a new job, he "hangs pictures." Hanging pictures sends a message that he believes that both he and his new management are completely committed to Torre's long-term success with the new organization. His "Rule #1" is: Create Mutual Respect and Trust." This is a big assumption considering that his boss was the volatile Yankee owner George Steinbrenner, who previously had gone through 21 different managers in 22 years. Steinbrenner's public tongue-lashings of former Yankee manager Billy Martin would also make Torre's assumption that he would be treated with respect and support seem naive. But Torre approached Steinbrenner with high expectations and has been more successful than his predecessors in working with this notorious boss. Sometimes, success is relative and Torre has been extremely successful relative to his predecessors. Although Torre is candid about the differences that Steinbrenner and he have had about the lineup, he is complimentary to his boss about three things during these differences.

1. Steinbrenner has not been as dictatorial as his reputation had indicated he would be. He lets Torre win his share.

2. Torre acknowledges that Steinbrenner is the boss.

3. Steinbrenner was often right in the changes he urged, and Torre made sure to acknowledge those times.

All of the above can serve as a strategy for viewing your relationships with your boss. First, your boss is just that—your boss, sometimes called your superior. Though words like boss or superior are not politically correct, don't delude yourself for a moment that the boss doesn't hold the power in your relationship. Acknowledging that the boss is the ultimate decision maker and that you are there to carry out the boss's strategies and wishes is the first step to winning in this area of office politics. Does this feel feudal or subservient? Get over it. Once you accept your second-in-command position, you can relax and look for more ways to succeed.

Second, add these phrases to your vocabulary when speaking to your boss.

- You were right.
- Congratulations.
- I'm sorry. I didn't realize that . . .
- Thank you for pointing that out. Can you help me . . .

Most bosses love to develop people who report to them. It's heady stuff for a boss to feel she can shape and re-create an employee into a new and improved professional. Allow your boss to constructively criticize you, coach you, go to bat for you, mentor you, and soon she will advance your career for you. Is this tough to swallow? As Joe Torre says, "Deal with it." You must accept the boss's prerogative to point out and polish your imperfections if you want to succeed in any organization.

Have you figured out one of the nice little perks of allowing your boss to take credit for honing your rough edges? When you do perform well, she will feel she participated in your success. She will want to point out your accomplishments.

Start looking for the things your boss does right. You can learn something from any boss. If the boss has no expertise to offer, why is she considered valuable to the company?

- visible community involvement
- skill at corporate politics
- stellar people skills
- successful through working with others

Tell your boss specifically what you notice that she has done well. You may drop this casually into a conversation or you may drop a note of congratulations if it's a deal closed or a case won.

In addition to this strategic approach, here's a list of must-do's for handling your boss.

TIPS FOR HANDLING YOUR BOSS

1. Communicate often with your boss in the style she prefers. If she likes casual conversations, learn her schedule and strike up a conversation at a time convenient for her. Does she prefer information in writing? Find an excuse to drop her positive notes on all sorts of subjects: notify her that you have completed a certain project; congratulate her on her presentation to her boss that was well received; pass along helpful information.

2. Know what your boss sees as your department's goals and how he prioritizes those goals. Management consultants sometimes do a revealing exercise with clients and their staffs. On Day One, they give the executive and his staff note cards. Each individual receives eight cards. All of them, including the executive, write down what they think the goals of the division or department are. At the end of Day One, the first revelation is that most of the staff don't know the goals of the executive. After much consternation, the executive then dictates the goals, with the helpful insights he has gained from the Day One exercise.

On Day Two, an even more interesting exercise takes place. The set of goals is given to the staff, but each goal is written on a separate note card. In other words, each staff member has a set of eight cards, a goal on each card. The staff is then asked to prioritize the goals of the department. Few people ever match in priority order with the executive providing leadership. It's not even close. Executives are astounded that people they work with daily don't understand the critical importance of certain goals over others.

You should always find out what your boss's priorities are for your department. Here are a few questions to ask:

◆ What is our department's most critical purpose for existence?
◆ What's the most important product or service we provide?
◆ What are the top three things we must accomplish this year?

Note: Be sure you know your department mission statement before you ask these questions. Tell your boss you are interested in her slant on things.

3. Ask for periodic performance reviews to help you improve. Get your boss involved in your professional development. If you are seeking your boss's advice and help in improving yourself professionally, she will have a personal stake in your success. She will want to acknowledge your improvement because she deserves part of the credit.

4. Invite your boss to participate in the good times in your career. Here are a few of the good times you can share with your boss:

◆ an appointment that will seal a deal with a major client. If it's a surefire done deal, share the spotlight with your boss.
◆ you are receiving an award or acknowledgment from a professional organization or service club
◆ you are viewing a cutting-edge or fun demonstration by a vendor

5. Impress your boss by being well informed.

◆ Read the same business magazines and books your boss does.

◆ Study your company's annual report and quote from it once in a while.

6. Use company money as if it were your own. Whether you are managing an expense account or buying supplies, be frugal and scrupulously honest with company funds. This gives the company a view of your integrity and shows you can be trusted with greater things.

7. Behave in a meeting as if your entire future depends on it; in part, it does.

   ◆ Act as if every word your boss says is fascinating. Give good eye contact, nod, and have an interested facial expression.
   ◆ Take notes.
   ◆ Always get there early.
   ◆ Don't be the cause of any interruption—cell phone vibrations, for example.

8. Take initiative. Offer to do things you probably will have to do anyway. Bosses love that because it's so refreshing. And don't shrink from unpleasant tasks. If the boss has asked you to do it, just do it. Always go around acting like a can-do, take charge go-getter. It's a winning image.

9. Never go over or around your boss. Your boss will still have the power to hurt you in the short term and you may be viewed to others as untrustworthy. And never ask your boss a question in public unless you are sure she knows the answer.

10. Avoid arguments. You never win an argument with a boss. You may win a point, but you may have to live with the long-term damage for years.

11. Admit your mistakes quickly. If you are 1 percent to blame for an error, take responsibility and ask for feedback on what your next move should be.

12. Know your boss's moods and quirks, and accommodate them. Some bosses are difficult to read. If they are angry, they may be just a little quieter than usual or they may seem preoccupied. Learn to pick up on your boss's mood and act accordingly.

    Most bosses want to be left alone; steer clear of them. Other bosses may find an excuse to meet with you because they want to vent. Be available. Learn to open up those communication lines. Don't choose that moment to keep your nose to the grindstone. Invite your boss in and offer your genuine interest and concern.

13. Also, be aware of little quirks. If you know your boss isn't a morning person, try not to communicate at all with her in the morning. Sharon Smith, a former management consultant, had a boss once who became very nervous driving over high bridges. Sharon and the rest of the staff had to drive with this boss to several locations throughout Louisiana. Over the bayous were some fairly high bridges. Sharon soon learned to anticipate when crossing a high bridge was on the agenda. She invented an excuse to drive on those days. She saved her boss the anxiety and embarrassment of revealing this problem to the staff. Sharon also won the support of her boss when a new position was created in the company, which Sharon eventually won. What are your boss's bridges? Quirks? Solve her problem.

14. Be a part of any of your boss's top initiatives. If your boss is addressing the Management Council, ask if you can attend to

help with handouts and for your professional development. If your boss is being inducted as president of the Rotary Club, offer to be her audience as she practices her inaugural address.

15. Become indispensable to your boss. Know where everything is and how to get things done. You will be the one the boss calls when he has to go out of town suddenly. He'll know he can count on you. You will also be his logical replacement when he is promoted.

16. Be a problem solver for your boss. By the time you go to your boss about a problem, you should have a solution or two already worked out. If not, you're a whiner. And remember, most problems evaporate if nothing is done. You probably don't even need to bother your boss with most problems. He will appreciate it.

17. Mirror your boss. Your boss has a style that she has come to believe is the right way to conduct business. You should mirror what she does. If she comes in early, at least once a week you should beat her to the office. If she stays late, mirror that. If she is very animated and energetic, don't slouch and slink

around the office. No matter how much work you put out, she will view you as lazy.

If she is formal in her language, you be formal. If she is casual and warm, be casual and warm. Learn her views and her work ethics, and emulate the ones you can with integrity.

18. Unclutter your office. Even bosses with messy desks often are critical of an employee's clutter. Clutter can be viewed as disorganization and brought up on a performance evaluation.

19. Make friends at work with people your boss views positively. This is especially true if you have a mentor. Your boss should in no way view the mentor as a threat or a negative influence.

20. Ask your boss for more responsibility. It's important to make sure that you cover your existing responsibilities first, however.

21. Laugh audibly at your boss's jokes unless they are offensive.

22. Maintain an even keel emotionally in front of your boss. Don't gush with excitement, act overly disappointed, or ever, *ever* get angry. Your boss will respect you more and admire your maturity. You will be viewed as reliable. Your demeanor should always be cheerful and upbeat, but not fawning. You should be a person your boss likes to run into in the hallway.

23. Tell big news and innovative ideas to your boss *before* you share them with anyone. Your boss should never be the second person to know anything you know.

24. Don't compare this boss to any boss you have had in the past. Remember, the "perfect boss" is a myth. Every boss has some things to offer you. Be open to new concepts or skills that this one can teach you.

25. Make friends with your boss's administrative assistant. Often, the assistant is the source of information the boss gets about his staff. He or she often determines who gets what time with the boss. You can get valuable clues to his moods and a heads up to a prejudice he may have about a certain project. Make an ally of this valuable person.

26. Let your boss know she is top priority. Don't put her on hold during a call. If she leaves you a message, return her call immediately—don't procrastinate. If she asks you if you have finished with a project and you haven't, speed up. She probably wants it now. Let her know in every way that pleasing her comes first; everything else is secondary.

27. Be ready for your boss's mistakes. He *will* make them. At times, even the best bosses treat employees unfairly. Whether through carelessness, lack of information, or pressure from sources you know nothing about, your boss will eventually treat you unfairly. Be prepared for how you will respond. Your response can be a turning point in your career. How you react can either solidify your relationship and increase your boss's respect for you, or a poor reaction can make an indelibly bad impression that will overshadow years of hard work.

If possible, take your medicine and let it drop. Weigh carefully if you even need to say anything to your boss.

If you feel you must say something, be sure to also let your boss know that you support the decision and accept it. Say something like, "Though I had hoped to be assigned the Xenidol account, I understand that you had good reasons to assign it to Frewick. Please let me know if I can help in any way."

28. Show gratitude for everything. Thank your boss for high marks on a performance review, feedback (even criticism) on a document you prepared, a great quarterly supervisors' meeting, and all the preparation involved, guiding your department through a perilous time.

"Thank you" is a phrase some managers hear rarely. You can motivate your boss and create an ally by saying these magic words.

29. Never correct or outshine your boss in the presence of others. You may be right in the content of what you say, but this would be a *dead wrong career move*. Not only could your boss harm your career in retaliation, other managers might think, "I would never hire that one. He might make me look bad in front of others, too."

30. Your purpose in the universe of your corporation is to make your boss successful. Make your boss look good and several things can happen.

◆ If your boss moves higher up the ladder, he is in a better position to move *you* up the ladder.

◆ Other executives may see the subtle way you loyally support your boss and the contributions you make. You may find yourself "stolen away" to a higher position. The key is to allow others to discover you; don't draw attention to the way you prop up your boss. That's counterproductive.

◆ Your boss may be so grateful that he supports you for a promotion, even if it means he loses you to another department. Though not all managers are this unselfish, this does happen. Remember, your boss is in a better position to know about upcoming job opportunities in the company than you are.

Your boss's recommendation could make you a shoo-in for a coveted position.

◆ Compensate for your boss's mistakes. Don't allow him to take all the consequences for his actions, even if he deserves what he gets. Protect and cover for him if it is possible and ethical to do so.

31. Always, *always* tell the truth, but don't be blunt. Gauge how much your boss really needs to know about a subject, tell what you must tell to maintain your integrity, and choose your words carefully and politically.

32. Don't waste your boss's time. Don't talk too much, don't run for help on trivial problems, don't *ever* get your boss involved in something she delegated to you, and don't make the boss repeat instructions. Handle everything you can to prove how responsible you are.

33. Never gossip.

34. Don't expose your boss to your personal problems. Present a picture to your boss that you are the master of interpersonal relationships. Protect your boss from having to deal with conflicts between your peers and you.

35. Remember dates and events that are special to your boss: birthdays, anniversaries of promotions, the ten-year anniversary with the company, completion of a personal or professional goal. Acknowledge with cards or flowers or tasteful, businesslike gifts like good pens or desk items. Learn the names of the boss's spouse, children, and close friends and relatives.

ACTION ITEMS

1. Write a note to your boss today with one of these messages.

   ◆ Thank the boss for help on a project or document or anything—even constructive criticism.
   ◆ Congratulate the boss on a successful meeting or presentation, a good idea, or her appointment to a prestigious
   committee.
   ◆ Pay your boss a professional compliment on a job well done
   that others might not have noticed.

2. Go to your boss and ask him to start working with you in an
   area that you would like to improve. Areas of improvement usually fall into two categories:

   ◆ *Technical.* These are skills that are required to perform the
   tasks of your job. Examples of things your boss may be qualified to help you with are new computer applications, departmental reports, the business plan, product knowledge.
   ◆ *Tactical.* Some bosses have less technical ability than you do.
   In that case, ask your boss to help you with the tactical parts
   of your job. Examples: handling irate clients, corporate etiquette, diplomatically saying "No" to other departments that
   want your services, networking to gain services from other
   departments, negotiating with vendors.

3. Quietly, start today to learn your boss's job. Learn all the crass
   operating details: what forms need to be filled out, the A.M. and
   P.M. routines, phone calls and contacts that must be done daily,
   and where everything is kept. This is part of your plot to become
   indispensable. You can glide right into the boss's chair when the
   spot comes open.

4. Analyze your boss's style, quirks, and patterns. If the boss is a morning person and you are not, force yourself to say a cheery "Hello" each morning. It won't be fatal. Is your boss a warm person and are you more aloof? Get in the habit of beginning every conversation with a statement that expresses interest in her.

Examples:

I hope your cold is better. You look like you had a good weekend. Did the dealership fix your car?

5. If your boss has a secretary, bring her a little something this week: a cup of Starbuck's coffee, a card, some pecan cookies that you baked. Tell her how you appreciate how she gives you a heads up occasionally on how to handle things, or tell her how you appreciate how pleasant she is to work with.

Chapter 4

How to Handle the World's Worst Bosses

Never look down on anybody unless you're helping them up.

—Jesse Jackson

No matter how politically skilled you are, you will eventually come across a boss who is difficult to handle. In a recent survey, many people said that there were more difficult bosses than supportive, competent bosses. What can you do to change them?

Nothing. When you leave that position for your next promotion, that boss will probably be just as cantankerous, just as ditzy, or just as impaired as the day you met him. You won't change him, but you can use his weaknesses to make yourself look fabulous. What a triumph in the organization's eyes! If your skills are seen to be strong enough to compensate for your boss's weakness, that makes you look even stronger.

An interesting note: Even if your company doesn't see that your skills are stronger than those of your boss, someone else may have noticed. Do you work with vendors, customers, or suppliers? At least 20 percent of the good job offers in recent years have come from sources like these outside your company. If a vendor tries to deal with you instead of your boss because she has learned that you grasp information quickly and are a strong decision maker, she may tell her boss, "We should hire this person." Sometimes companies even offer employees cash incentives to identify good hiring prospects.

One note of caution: Our feelings are tricky. We may *feel* we have a bad boss when really we have a temporary problem or may even be part of the problem ourselves. Wait it out. Be very sure you have a bad boss before proceeding with the strategies below.

Most bad bosses fit into one of the following categories. Some bosses are combinations of two or three of these unflattering categories.

THE "I'M A STAR AND YOU'RE NOT" BOSS

(Includes the Competitive Boss)

You have heard the comments:

"He's a legend in his own mind."
"If you want to know how great she is, just ask her."
"He was breaking his arm patting himself on the back."

Egos

Some egos are so large they leave no room for the egos of others. Bosses in this category are obsessed with keeping the corporate spotlight focused on themselves. The word "share" is not in their vocabularies.

Other bosses who fit in this category may surprise you. They may not come across as bragging or power hungry or arrogant. In fact, they may have been great bosses to work for—until you started showing a little star quality of your own.

You may have first noticed the strange behavior of this boss when you successfully completed a project that drew praise or interest from others. Because you report to your boss, she may have accepted the compliments with little mention of your input, hard work, or the simple fact that you deserved most of the credit. Instead, she extolled the virtues of the project, how valuable it was, the steps that were taken to make the project a success—everything except your name. By discussing the merits of the project, the boss gave the impression she played a much greater role in making things happen than she did. She isn't lying; she's just leaving out an important element—you.

A boss like this one may be supportive of you one on one. She may even get you salary hikes and promotions. Yet she makes it very clear that only one star can exist in a department and that you are not it. She is the point person, the quarterback, the front-runner. If you were a club, she would be the president. If you were flying a plane, she would be the pilot. And if you were bees, you would be a drone and she would be the queen. You get the picture.

THE THREATENED AND COMPETITIVE BOSS

This boss rationalizes that she is responsible for anything you produce; therefore, the accomplishment really is hers. She may view herself as the visionary, the overseer, and you are just a pair of hands—the praise really should go to her. The boss is threatened that you might expose her lack of imagination or diligence by revealing that she did not contribute much to the project.

A threatened boss is a dangerous boss. Her tactics could be harmful to your career. Isn't it ironic that your reward for excellence is that your boss may try to (consciously or unconsciously) discredit you?

Here are a few of the ways these bosses steal from you:

◆ leaving you out of meetings where your project/idea is presented
◆ telling you to let her do the talking in meetings if your idea/ project is presented.
◆ using patronizing or demeaning language to belittle your role.

Examples:

The boss says: Sherry was part of my team who helped me produce this event.

> *Translation: Sherry was the team that produced the entire event.*

I appreciate Sherry's input on the project.

> *Translation: Sherry's input amounted to 100 percent of the project, but I'm making it sound like 1 percent.*

◆ putting their own name prominently on a title page or introductory slide or anything that announces authorship or project responsibility.

◆ telling you that your idea/project isn't good, then reworking it only slightly and taking full credit. (Bosses like this convince themselves that the minor tweaking they did created something new. *Not!*)

◆ always saying, "I did this" or "I did that" when really you or a teammate did the actual work

◆ in reality, not working as a team. Oh yes, lip service will be given to being team members, but this boss never lets you forget that she's the lead dog and it's your job to watch her rear

◆ scheduling you so that you are not around for tours, executive visits, or other opportunities to take appropriate credit

◆ competing. "Anything you can do, I can do better" are the words to a song from *Annie Get Your Gun*. You may begin to feel that it's your boss's theme song if he becomes consciously or unconsciously competitive with you. The competitive boss is often unconsciously competing. Some competitive bosses feel that they are stretching you by trumping everything you do. Whatever the motivation, the first step is to identify whether you have a competitive boss. A competitive boss may

    – give you a letter to write, then write her own letter and compare the two. Guess whose letter is deemed best?

    – ask for your ideas, then say "No, this is the way it is" or "This is better." Again, her idea will trump your idea every time.

    – point out your shortcomings jokingly to others, especially if you are receiving praise.

    – compete in nonwork arenas: sports, purchases, accomplishments.

    – say a lot of things like, "When I was your age ..." or "When I was in sales . . . ."

Interestingly enough, a competitive boss may really be a strong fan and ally of yours. Some bosses only feel competitive with an employee whom they respect. Keep this in mind when considering whether you really need to do anything at all. As long as the competition stays friendly, you may actually benefit from these silly games.

Strategies

1. Always create your own impressive cover sheet or cover letter that includes your name. Send this out with any information or paraphernalia related to the project. It may be wise to include your boss's name, also.

Project Outline

NEW EMPLOYEE ORIENTATION PROJECT

Designed by

Luanne Taylor

January 30, 2008

Phone: 123-4444

Fax: 123-4445

Ellen Barksdale, Manager

Department of Professional Development

---

2. When you see your boss's boss or other influential people, let them know what you're achieving. If you see your boss's boss at

the elevator, he may say, "How are you?" Instead of just saying, "Fine," use this opportunity. Say something like, "I've almost completed the Fillmore Project."

3. When you meet one on one with your boss, be very deferential. In private, you can be as subservient to the boss as he might want. Stroke this needy ego by functioning as the minion he fantasizes you are. It can only help to make him feel secure with you. The last thing you want is for him to feel that your ego is too big to bow down to his ego.

4. Learn to drop carefully phrased comments into conversations, presentations, and meetings. These phrases should accomplish two goals.

- ◆ Compliment but realistically define your boss's limited input.
- ◆ Give an honest assessment of what you have contributed.

Example:

You might say: Although this has been my pet project for two months, I have to give credit to Barbara for giving me the assignment.

5. Praise, praise, praise. You can't praise a boss like this too much. Just because you would find such self-serving flattery a turnoff, don't think that your boss will. This is one embarrassingly simplistic move that never ceases to amaze me because it is so effective. The best compliments are tied to specific events because they sound sincere.

Examples:

I couldn't help overhearing you on the phone with Mr. Belden. How did you learn those political skills? Can you teach me?

You really headed off that problem in the meeting by asking Jim to talk about next month's sales meeting. Do you plan strategic moves like that or have you always had good instincts? Do you think that's something I could learn? How did you start?

6. Sometimes, you have to let the boss win one—even if he doesn't deserve it. Occasionally, allow the boss to take credit and don't pipe up. These little "gifts" will improve your relationship and, with most people, decrease the competitive element.

7. Script your boss in a subtle way. Go into your boss early in a project (before he has had time to steal the credit). Plant key phrases about your work in your boss's mind. She just might wind up saying these phrases when she discusses the project with others. This is the power of suggestion, and it frequently works.

Examples:

> *Ron, thank you for entrusting me with my first* **solo project.** *You have contributed the vision, and I just want to tell you that I plan to manage, execute, and deliver this project since you have* **given me the responsibility.** *At the end, I want you to feel that I merited your confidence because I* **was able to take your idea and run with it.** *I've had managers who couldn't delegate, but you* **do it intelligently.** *I think the whole department benefits.*

Phrases like **solo project, take your idea and run with it,** and **delegate intelligently** may pop up in your boss's conversations with others. In other words, he is telling others that you did the project.

8. Competitive bosses require special handling. The first thing you have to get under control is your own defensiveness. Don't feel that you have to respond to your boss's competitive behavior. Here are just a few of the reasons that defending yourself may be a bad idea.

   ◆ Your boss really isn't listening to how good you are because she's too busy believing her own press.
   ◆ She may think you're exaggerating.
   ◆ She may not have seen her own competitive behavior but she's sure to notice yours!

   Why not let the boss win the competition? She'll be happier and easier to deal with. If she gets all those strokes, she'll feel more comfortable patting you on the back, maybe even in front of others.

Perhaps the most difficult thing you will have to do in dealing with a boss like this is to keep your emotions on an even keel. No one enjoys being treated like a second-class citizen. A star boss almost thinks he has been born of a race of superheroes, that he's not a plebeian like you. Keep your cool. Keep on keeping on. Eventually, there is justice in the business world.

THE FORMER MENTOR YOU HAVE SURPASSED

Sometimes a person who has been your greatest supporter cannot handle your new success. Your former boss may have difficulty

◆ asking or accepting direction from *you.*
◆ requesting permission, resources, or favors *from you.*
◆ treating you like the seasoned, experienced professional you are.

The truth is that some people are at their best in the helping role but can't *accept* help as graciously. These individuals are the best allies of those at the bottom rungs of the corporate ladder. As mentors, these bosses will go out on a limb to get training funds or to trust lower-level employees with greater, more prestigious responsibilities. These bosses are rare and valuable to those getting started. Unfortunately, this type can be downright difficult when an employee rises to become equal or even superior in position.

Suddenly, the boss is not in a role of helping, which is a position of power! If the former employee is now equal to the boss, the balance of power has shifted. Who has lost power? The boss. This can leave some people feeling deflated, and they may look at you critically. They may begin to have thoughts like these:

> My former employee has really let her promotion go to her head.
> He was a nice guy, but now he has changed.
> Some people just can't handle authority.

Your former boss may have issues about any one of the following.

◆ His own career is stalled; your moving up the ladder has made him aware of his own lack of momentum.

◆ She may have had a hurtful past experience with an employee she has mentored. Backstabbing those who made you is not unheard of in large corporations.

◆ He may be worried about confidences or business practices he shared with you when you were under his control. Now, you are not. If your boss always bad-mouthed Human Resources and your new position is Assistant Director of Human Resources, your old boss may be nervous.

Strategies

1. The first step is defining exactly what your problem is. That means communicating honestly—but carefully—with your former boss.

Examples:

Stage 1—As soon as you are promoted, call him and give him credit. Encourage him to share your success. Say right out loud, "I hope we will continue to have a good working relationship. With this promotion, I value you more than ever. Although things may be different in some ways, one thing won't change: the respect I have for you."

Stage 2—If a few hints of negativity have come your way, make an appointment to see your former boss. Taking the boss to lunch is usually best so the feeling of camaraderie is enhanced. Do not accuse or point out anything you feel your former boss has done. At this point, that would be a mistake. After some pleasant conversation about work, families, hobbies, or current events, say something like the following:

I don't know if I have ever acknowledged to you that I owe you a lot for helping put me in this position. When I think about _____ and _____ (fill in the blank with two specific things your boss did for you), then I am truly grateful.

or

I'm going to need a lot of help and support in this new position. I'd like to feel I can still call you from time to time to get your take on things. I have benefited from your experience in the past. Many things have changed but I hope I can still count on you to help me.

2. Try to break the ice by looking for excuses to collaborate with your old boss. Try to work together on committees, focus groups, or a common task like writing annual goals.

3. Most strategies for the "I'm a Star and You're Not" boss will work here.

THE PARENTAL BOSS

What is a parental boss? A parental boss displays many of the behaviors the parent of a young child may display. He or she is usually a micromanager. Here are some characteristics:

◆ He tells you what to do; doesn't care a lot about asking your input.

◆ She judges that you're a good employee/bad employee by whether you have done exactly what you were told immediately. The parental boss is less interested in the results you get than in whether you did what you were told.

◆ He can't let go of responsibility. The parental boss may hover while you are doing your work. This boss fears that you will make a mistake unless you are carefully supervised.

◆ You can hear lots of evaluative statements peppered throughout this boss's conversation:
  – That's good.
  – Oh, no.
  – That's not right.
  – Right.

◆ The boss may feel comfortable fussing at you or chewing you out—even publicly.
◆ The boss acts like a sugar daddy with company resources. He bestows perks, plum assignments, and raises as though they are gifts given personally by him.

Strategies

1. The next time you and your boss sit down to set goals for you, tell her you feel strongly that the next step in your professional development is for you to either

   ◆ take on more responsibility, or
   ◆ develop a more proactive approach to your work.

   Then tell her that you would like to do the next project/task with almost complete autonomy. Choose a low-risk, low-profile project/task for this experiment. Ask if you can do the project alone, with only one or two checkpoints for her input. Establish when those checkpoints will be: At the project's beginning? Middle? End? Before money is invested? Before a hiring decision is made? Do a good job and the boss may do more projects like this.

2. This one is risky. Proceed at your own peril only if you can no longer stand being publicly berated. Ask for an appointment to talk about a personal issue. Be sure the appointment is on a day and at a time that the boss is most likely to be unstressed and undistracted. Say something like the following:

   I have come to ask your help with a problem. You know that I like working for you because [you know the   business better than anyone] [you are willing to invest in your people]. (Fill in with your boss's strengths.)

I am having difficulty, however, going through the process of being publicly criticized as I was when I made the error on the Hemphill file. You were completely right to criticize me. I learned from it. But it's the public part and the way you talked to me that are difficult for me.

I want us to have a good working relationship. I'm willing to try to change things I'm doing wrong and improve. In fact, I very much want to. I'd like for us to find a way to communicate about these things. Do you have any suggestions?

Hopefully, your boss will offer to stop publicly criticizing you. If not, you may want to ask her to stop like this.

Do you think that we could communicate about my mistakes in private from now on?

3. Don't encourage the parent/child dynamic. Not even jokingly should you engage in childlike antics like hiding things from the boss as if you are afraid, asking for favors in a wheedling way, or acting as if the boss owns the resources of the company and that he is doling them out like sweets to a child.

Parental bosses often act as if raises or bonuses or days off are gifts from them personally. That is not a healthy attitude. These are company resources. Although you should express appreciation for the allocation of these things, don't behave as if you have received these for getting on the boss's good side. That's an unpredictable emotional roller coaster.

THE QUIXOTIC BOSS

Although bosses like this may not seem to be difficult to others, they can be the most challenging to work for. A person who constantly changes her mind may seem creative and spontaneous, but this behavior gets mighty old mighty fast when you have to work together every day.

Here's a typical scenario. Let's say your boss, Harry, comes in all excited on Monday morning with a new plan for the professional development of every employee in the department. He says to you, "Art, an article I read over the weekend made me realize that the key to our department's thriving during the upcoming changes in our company is to train our people. I want to initiate a full-scale project to make our department the best-trained group in the company, and I want you to head it up. This is my top priority."

You spend Tuesday through Thursday researching seminars, training consultants, corporate coaches, and evaluation instruments.

On Friday, he asks you how much headway you have made on a totally different project—the business plan. You confidently say that you have temporarily put that aside to devote more time to getting the training project off to a successful start.

Harry looks at you sort of puzzled, then a light begins dawning in his eyes. He then looks at you sympathetically as if you're a bit slow and says, "I know you're really excited about that project, and, of course, development is important, but the business plan is a top priority."

Say what? How can Harry not know that just a few days ago he said that the professional development project was a top priority?

You and I will never understand how things a quixotic boss has said can fly completely out of his mind, evaporate, self-erase. Suffice it to say that it can and does happen.

Even if you tediously went back over the conversation, the quixotic boss probably wouldn't remember saying what he said. Don't even go there. There are no rewards for you in winning that battle.

Strategies

1. Keep a paper trail. E-mail your boss and ask him to fill in the blank question about what he wants you to do.

    Example:

    Do you want me to postpone my work on the business plan for a couple of weeks and work full time on the professional development project?

2. Check in frequently with your boss. Look for clues that he has changed directions so that you can change yours. This checking in can save you hours and weeks of wasted work. For example, if your boss likes to chat over coffee in the morning, briefly and casually drop into the conversation what you have on your agenda for the day. If your boss wants to change the agenda, he has the opportunity.

3. Copy your boss on everything. If you have received confirmation from a hotel that you can have the main ballroom for the kick-off of your professional development project, copy your boss. At the top of the confirmation write, "Good News. We got the large space we wanted for the kickoff of the professional development project. We're on our way!"

4. For even an informal meeting, bring a typed agenda with your projects on it.

5. Periodically, ask your boss to sit down with you to clarify priorities. Bring a list of your current initiatives. Say something like, "We have several initiatives going right now. How would you rank them in urgency or importance?"

THE IMPAIRED BOSS

If you have enough bosses in your career, you will eventually have a boss who is impaired. The impairment may be temporary or permanent. Here are some of the most familiar ways people become impaired on the job.

- ◆ alcohol

- ◆ prescription drugs

- ◆ illness

- ◆ sleep deprivation

- ◆ emotional or psychological problems

- ◆ distracting marital or family problems

- ◆ depression or anxiety

- ◆ hardening of the arteries, low/high blood sugar, Alzheimer's, serious disease

◆ anxiety   ◆ grief (death, divorce, empty-
                             nest syndrome)

How do you deal with a boss whose behavior becomes erratic or substandard? For one thing, be careful to ask yourself if the boss's behavior is truly unacceptable.

Strategies

What if there is no doubt that the impairment is a problem?

1. Proceed cautiously. In most cases, you do not want to be the one to acknowledge the problem first. If at all possible, allow someone else to blow the whistle. Being the one to name names may have all kinds of consequences for your career—not to mention legal ones. Attempt to put your boss in situations that will force one of the following people to see and deal with the impairment:

   ◆ your boss's boss
   ◆ someone close to your boss in the company
   ◆ your boss's last boss
   ◆ a psychologist, counselor, human resources representative

2. Avoidance is sometimes the most politically astute move for your career. Transfer to another department rather than put yourself in the center of a controversy. Some large corporations have a code of silence about impairment, particularly alcoholism. Although the corporation may not approve of your boss's behavior, it may not like whistle blowers either.

3. Keli, a young stockbroker, tells about a respected broker who drank heavily each day at lunch. Everyone in the company knew it, and Keli knew it after only a few weeks on the job; he got

testy when he drank. Keli learned quickly to avoid him at all costs after lunch. Because he had loyal old customers who brought in millions in revenue for the company, management would never fire him.

Keli's solution was to hold the phone to her ear even if the line were dead when she saw him stumbling toward her desk in the afternoon.

Learning to work around impaired people is an acquired skill. Sometimes it's the best tactic. Here are some tips for practicing avoidance.

◆ Learn the impaired boss's schedule. Learn his highs and lows. When are his most alert, constructive times of day? Plan to communicate only in that window when the boss is functioning best.

◆ Would it be better to communicate with your boss in front of others? Some impaired bosses will muster up the ability to function adequately if more than one person is present. Take a coworker with you to discuss a project. Your boss may feel the need to pull herself together for even an audience of two.

◆ Communicate by e-mail or memo. An impaired boss may wait to answer correspondence until he is functioning better. Also, you will have a record if you suffer because of his impaired judgment.

◆ Secretly leave AA material or the card of a counselor on her desk or where she can find it.

4. This is the last resort. If you fear you may be abetting unacceptable, unsafe, or even criminal behavior by not speaking up, then you may have to do so. If at all possible, meet with your boss first. Give your boss the opportunity to seek treatment on his own. You might say something like this:

I have something difficult to talk about so I'm going to ask you to hear me out. You may not agree with what I'm about to say, but for the sake of the department will you agree to give me five uninterrupted minutes?

Then:

We have worked together on several situations lately that have been affected by decisions that really don't seem like the Harry Smith that I have worked with for two years. Are you going through a difficult time or is there something going on with you?

Give the boss a chance to discuss his problem. The ideal situation is for the boss to bring up the alcohol or problem himself. If not, proceed with a very brief objective description of the problems or errors your boss has caused due to the dysfunction. Ask your boss if you can do anything to help. Many bosses will take the hint and get help—they know that if you have noticed, others will too.

If not, express your concerns. Say something like, "I feel that I may put the project and my job in jeopardy if this happens again. I am very concerned. You should be concerned because this move may, in fact, put *your* job in jeopardy." Hopefully, your boss will take the hint.

THE NEW OR INEXPERIENCED BOSS

What do you do when your boss has less experience than you do? The boss, whether due to youth or the newness of his assignment, may lack the experience you would have hoped he would have.

The inexperience may be in the technology, operations, or knowledge of your particular department. More often, the lack of experience is in the management side of the business: communicating, reading people, delegating, or other people-related issues.

As Baby Boomers age and leave companies, you will see more and more inexperienced bosses; after all, the best bosses in the world were once in this category. How can you work with this type of boss so that your time together is a success for both of you?

Strategies

1. Find ways to acknowledge the experience these bosses do have. Ask them about previous jobs, internships, and accomplishments. Give them an opportunity to tell you about their past, no matter how brief.

2. Ask for their help. Tell them that you would like to learn more about e-commerce, doing business in China, computer graphics, or anything that they know something about. Put them in the role of mentor before you subtly mentor them.

3. Prepare well for your first meeting or conversation with your new boss. Learn her strengths, her major, her degrees, her previous experience, and what management saw in her that made her valuable to your department.

   At the first meeting, let her do most of the talking. Don't overwhelm her with your ideas or who you are. Convey that you are pleased that she was selected to head up your group. At some point say, "Please let me know if I can make your transition easier in any way."

4. Only after you do Strategies 1, 2 and 3 do you proceed with 4. Carefully, offer to be a resource to your new boss. Acknowledge the good things you have seen her do. Tell her you like what you see and that you want to be a contributing member of her team. Offer to help in any way you can. Don't, under any circumstances, allude to her youth, lack of experience, or lack of technical knowledge. Don't make comparative statements like, "Since I've been working here for so long (implying she hasn't), I can offer you some pointers."

5. If your boss is really failing to do some important things because she is unaware these things should be done, set up a one-on-one meeting. Make a list of the things you think need to be done but call them "suggestions." Begin the meeting by saying, "Since you have delegated the national accounts to me, I have spent some time thinking about making my area function more efficiently. I have put together the following suggestions. I'd appreciate your feedback since some of these are dependent on your support."

6. If your boss is making errors, take these steps.

   ◆ Don't say anything.
   ◆ Continue to not say anything.
   ◆ Have a private conversation with your boss. Try to act as if this topic just casually pops up. Begin the conversation with a specific example of something the boss has done recently that you think went extremely wrong. Casually say, "Did you know that the Activity Report is due on the first of the month and not the fifteenth? Why that report is out of sync with the others, I don't know, but I thought you'd want to know."

7. Find ways to educate your boss. Here are some suggested comments.

I don't know how you're learning about pressurized sealants so quickly. I never could have learned it without going to those seminars sponsored by ASI.

Would you like to see my latest newsletter from ASI? There is a great article on the boiling points of pitch sealants. (Or route it through the department.)

What book? Oh, this humongous book on my desk? That's just a reference book I refer to from time to time to look up information on various sealants. I would have made some catastrophic mistakes without it.

THE INCOMPETENT BOSS

Somehow, certain people are able to rise to positions of responsibility for which they have no qualifications or abilities. When you find you work for an incompetent boss, you will have to quickly pass through that phase of bewilderment about how your company could have overlooked such ineptness and given this person the role of being your boss.

Here are the five stages you will go through when you discover you are working for an incompetent boss.

1. bewilderment

2. dismay

3. anger

4. resignation and acceptance

5. proactivity

Stage 1—**Bewilderment.** At first you think maybe you have missed something or that your boss is temporarily distracted. As your boss commits blunder after blunder, you realize he really is incompetent.

Stage 2—**Dismay.** Please waste no time on this phase. It's not productive. In Stage 2, you are horrified that no one who interviewed him or worked with him picked up on his gross stupidity. You feel like the only soul who can see that the emperor is wearing no clothes. Still, if you run around wringing your hands and exclaiming over this sorry state of affairs, you will be viewed as negatively as the incompetent boss.

Stage 3—**Anger.** Anger sets in because incompetent bosses create problems like the following for people like you.

- ◆ You have to do part of their job as well as yours.
- ◆ They mess up things you have already done.
- ◆ They block you from marketing your talents to the rest of the organization.
- ◆ You can look bad through guilt by association.

◆ You're probably not free to defend yourself because the boss holds your performance review, promotions, and even your job security in his helpless little hands. Frustrating.

Stage 4—**Resignation and Acceptance.** You accept that you're stuck with the boss and stop investing energy in rebelling against the situation. You decide to either wait out the situation or take action. Waiting it out is usually best. The boss will transfer, or, as you may be even more dismayed to see, be promoted. In a few happy situations, the boss's incompetence catches up and he is fired.

Or, your circumstances could change. You could transfer or be promoted thanks to your incompetent but supportive boss.

Stage 5—**Proactivity.** Proactivity is the stage in which you take control of your destiny again. You decide that you can't change your boss, but that you can make some good things happen for yourself. The strategies below will help you in dealing with your incompetent boss in a proactive way.

Strategies

1. Be sure you have reviewed the five stages above. This will help you avoid many of the mistakes that could hurt you more than they hurt your boss. Also review the strategies under "The New or Inexperienced Boss."

2. Join every focus group and committee you can find in your company. You need to display your competency. If others see how

proficient and able you are, they will soon figure out that the incompetency in your department is not coming from you.

3. Volunteer to work on projects that will expose you to your boss's boss or peer group.

4. Copy others on the work you do. Don't go over your boss's head, but copy anyone you legitimately feel should be kept informed.

5. Drop compliments on your boss's work that are really coded messages separating her work from yours.

Examples:
I got the research to Martha only last Thursday and she had written the entire report by Monday.

This is code language for:

I did every bit of the research myself. That sloppy, error-filled report was the sole work product of Martha, who didn't put much time into it.

6. Work around your boss's incompetencies. Find those two or three things the boss does well and keep her busy doing those things. You and your peers may have to pick up the slack. Sometimes to succeed you have to compensate for a weak link like your boss.

Let's say that your boss is a poor presenter. Her presentations to other departments are an embarrassment. Here are some examples of diplomatic ways to get your boss to allow you to take over.

For me to develop my presentation skills, I need to be challenging myself now. May I do one of the interdepartmental briefings you have coming up?

I have a good relationship with the Accounting Department. If you ever want me to handle their briefing I would be pleased to help.

THE UNPOPULAR BOSS

You have a boss that almost no one in the company likes. He has no influence, no allies, no power base. Only through persistence and dumb luck has he attained his position. And you are associated with him. When they think of your department, they visualize this person and you as his cohort. You must act to make sure people see that you are on his staff but definitely not his clone.

Strategies

1. Do your best to speak well of your boss. Never, never, *never* whine or backstab. You will be the last person any other boss will want to hire if you speak ill of your boss—even if everyone knows he deserves it.

   Don't defend your boss or argue that he is right. He probably isn't. Still, you can use these phrases when others complain about the things your boss has done.

   I'm sure Jerry didn't mean to come across that way. I'll talk to him, and we'll work out something for you.

   We ought to be able to do that for you. I'll take this information back to Jerry. He'll probably see it differently once he reviews this information.

I am sorry so much of your time went into this and then it was not used. That would disappoint me, too. We will be more attentive to our scheduling in the future.

2. Send out a memo telling other departments what you *can* do for them. Use phrases like "XYZ Department wants to support you in the following ways."

3. Attend any meeting or social function the company sponsors. Allow people to get to know you one on one.

4. Follow strategies for "The Incompetent Boss." Your boss is incompetent in interpersonal relationship skills.

THE BOSS WHO DOESN'T KEEP HER PROMISES

Beth is very generous with her promises. She tells her employees she will put their names up for promotion, give them comp time for extra hours worked, requisition new computers for them, and get paperwork turned around faster so that her desk isn't their bottleneck. But these promises are rarely kept. Beth gives a great pep talk and sounds earnest in her assurances. These assurances, however, are meaningless.

She forgets, or something comes up, or budget crunches force her to withdraw a recommendation. It's always something. The problem is, Beth was so urgent and convincing when she used her promise to inspire her people that they remember vividly that she gave her word.

Credibility is one of the most important foundations of good management, and broken promises destroy credibility. A boss destroys any confidence or respect an employee has for her if her word is not good.

Strategies

1. When your boss promises you something, attempt to get it in writing. E-mail the boss right after the conversation. Say, "Thank you for agreeing to replace my old computer. Should I review the PCs on the market or will you be making that choice?"

   Somehow phrase the question so that the boss is acknowledging that she said you would receive a new computer. Also, phrase it so that her reply and confirmation are required.

2. Build the promised equipment or event into your annual goals and objectives.

   Examples:

   ◆ Learn to operate your new PC to the extent that you can turn out my weekly report in under an hour.
   ◆ After attending the National Conference in July, conduct a staff meeting to share the information with your peers.

3. Create a timeline. If your boss has said she will promote you in November, create a timeline, starting with today's date. Let's say it's May. Your timeline could look like this.

May	June	July	August	Sept	Oct	Nov
Begin Plan for Promotion	Review Promotion Preparations with Manager	Cross-train Ellen to take my Position	Review Transition Needs with Manager	Wrap Up Projects in Current Position	Order New Business Cards	Promotion

Review this timeline with your manager. You'll notice there are several built-in opportunities to remind her of her promise.

4. Immediately after your boss tells you she will promote you, mention it within earshot of her boss or her peers if this is appropriate. Say something like this.

I appreciate the opportunity Dana is giving me by supporting my promotion. I just wanted to let you know how pleased I am to be with a company that acknowledges the people within.

(Be careful with this one. If you have a nagging feeling that your boss may want to be the first to tell *her* boss that she is promoting you, then don't implement this strategy.)

5. Another last resort: If you're going to resign anyway, go to your boss and tell her that you have a better offer at another firm. Tell her that they are able to give you the position you are seeking from your present company. (Be sure this is true!)

Rather than lose you, she may come back with a counteroffer. It is not uncommon to receive more from bosses after resigning than you have ever received from them when they thought you wouldn't leave them.

Don't bluff, however. You may find yourself with no job at all.

6. If your boss promises you a resource to motivate you to accept a project, and then fails to provide the resource, put the ball back in her court. Get her involved in problem solving with you. After all, she has created the problem that will keep you from meeting the deadline. Say something like the following:

I need your help. Since we're not going to be able to afford the new copier that collates and staples, I have been coming up with ways we might still be able to complete the employee handbooks by year-end. Any one of these options will help us get the job done without purchasing the new copier—at least for right now. Which is doable from your perspective?

◆ Outsource the work to Kinko's.
◆ Hire a temp for two days to hand-collate.
◆ Tell the VP that due to equipment problems our handbook delivery date has been postponed.

When faced with these options, there's a chance you might get that copier after all, or at least a little help. There's always a risk, however. Bosses like this can be defensive, so listen to that voice within that tells you whether or not this is an acceptable risk for you to take.

THE UNAVAILABLE BOSS AND THE POOR COMMUNICATOR

A boss can make himself unavailable in so many ways:

◆ always being in meetings
◆ not communicating well
◆ closing his door to work
◆ having a thousand rules about when you can approach him and when you can't

Examples:
He says, "Never bother me before 10:00 in the morning."
He travels, goes to conferences, meets with customers/vendors outside the office.
He makes you feel guilty for approaching him by saying, "That's why I delegated that to you."

Strategies

1. Schedule time well in advance with your boss.

2. Listen to what your boss has told you about the best times to meet with him. If he has said that mornings are out and you've observed that his attention span gets short at around 5:00 P.M., check in with him at around 2:00 P.M.

3. In your next meeting with your boss, tell him that you would like to know what time of day is best for him to answer questions or meet. Say, "I know mornings are your time to complete managerial tasks, so could you tell me the best time for me to drop by for approvals or to run ideas by you? I don't want to interrupt."

4. Be sure that you are not scheduling frivolous meetings. Resolve to approach the boss only if it is absolutely unavoidable. If the boss knows you only try to get in to see him when there's a real need, he'll be more likely to be available.

5. Determine your boss's favorite mode of communication:

   ◆ face-to-face and one-on-one
   ◆ meetings of three or more
   ◆ e-mails
   ◆ memos
   ◆ formal presentations
   ◆ casual conversations in the hall
   ◆ his office, his turf
   ◆ your office, so he can get away if he needs to

After you have observed him and decided what his preferences are, cater your communication to him. If he is uncooperative about scheduling appointments but will come into your office with a coffee mug on Monday morning, you should be sitting there waiting for him every Monday. Even the poorest communicators have their moments when they're slightly better than at other times.

THE YELLER

Some bosses just yell. Their first boss probably yelled and they think that's acceptable. In their minds, that's what managers do when they're driving home a point.

Believe it or not, some of the yellers are surprised to find that you take it personally. They feel that being yelled at is just part of paying your dues.

Some yellers are, in fact, great bosses in every other way. They're fair, ethical, supportive, generous, and knowledgeable. Their only problem is their volume and their volatility.

Strategies

1. Schedule a time to meet with your boss when she is in a good mood. If at all possible, bring her a completed project or good news to begin the meeting on a positive note.

   Whatever you do, don't use judgmental tones or words that evaluate her style. Instead, approach this as a dual challenge that the two of you need to work out.

Example:

I know styles differ from person to person. I know I may be a bit quiet [uncommunicative, reserved] for some people's taste. I believe that I could do a better job for you if we communicated better. Maybe it's my response, but I can't think productively when you raise your voice when we're talking. Can you work with me to help resolve this problem? I don't want it to affect our relationship or our work product.

2. Work it into your next performance review. In assessing your own performance, first mention some areas for which you are responsible: better time management, delegation, organization. Next, tell your boss you think that your performance would improve dramatically if the two of you could improve your communication.

3. Only in cases of extreme abuse should you talk to anyone other than your boss: senior management, a Human Resources representative, or even peers. Even if you are justified, taking this route can be very painful for you and can follow you when you apply for jobs in the future. People who are hiring fear problems from someone who has "officially" had a problem with a former boss.

   If the situation is really bad, consider a transfer or a new job as an alternative to abusive treatment.

THE PASSIVE BOSS

He listens. He's not stupid. He does what's required of him. Here's what he *doesn't* do:

◆ take the lead
◆ see opportunities for your department
◆ give you a heads up when you need it
◆ make timely decisions
◆ champion his people (or even adequately represent them)
◆ ask *his* boss for things the department needs (budget, personnel, and the like)

Not only does your boss not want to rock the boat, he won't even row forward a little bit.

Strategies

1. The more you directly push a passive boss, the more doggedly he resists. You must proceed obliquely. Don't speak or act too boldly. Begin conversations with questions or by asking his views on your topic. Don't try to pin him down. You may not even want to bring up your request in the first conversation. Take it slow and easy.

2. Find out what he likes, what he believes in, and what feels safe to him. For example, if he feels more comfortable with lots of documentation, bury him in documentation. If he likes things simple, make your premise downright elementary.

Example:

If we add that employee, we'll bring in an additional $300,000 a year. If we don't, we'll barely be profitable.

3. Pare down what you ask for. Make your requests few and far between. This type hates to be put on the spot and will view you negatively if you ask too often.

4. Passive bosses find safety in numbers. If you are trying to get him to create a position and add another marketing rep, try this. Tell him how Joe Smith in Accounting has added three new staff members and Jerald Ivey in Human Resources has recently added two. Hint that not growing his staff looks a little conspicuous since growth is going on everywhere else. This may work.

5. Try the strategies for "The Incompetent Boss."

6. If your boss doesn't want to take risks, find out if he will object to your taking the risks. If he doesn't want to ask for an extra marketing rep for your department, put together an outstanding business case with your name on it. Ask if he will pass it along.

ACTION ITEMS

1. The first step is to determine if you have a bad boss. Maybe the problem is a misunderstanding. Maybe the problem is due to her being new on the job. Maybe the problem is you.

   Ask a trusted friend or two outside the company to help you decide if the problem could have a justifiable reason. If you decide you do have a problem boss, proceed to Step 2.

2. Determine which type of problem boss you have. Review the various types. You may have a combination of two or three. Review the steps for each.

Your next three Action Items will depend on the type of boss you have. List steps below that you think are the most appropriate ones for you to take right away. You may want to do others later.

3. _____

4. _____

5. _____

Chapter 5

The Art of Dirty Politics: Fighting Back

If life was fair, Elvis would be alive and all the impersonators would be dead.

—Johnny Carson

Have you ever been the victim of dirty politics? It's a painful experience and the memory lingers forever. Feelings of frustration, helplessness, anger, and bitterness may be intense. Perhaps that's why when the term "office politics" is mentioned, what springs to mind for most people is the dirty tricks brand of politics.

There is no denying that dirty politics exist in business. I believe, however, that the practice of dirty politics is rarer than most people believe. The problem is that those dirty tricks draw lots of attention and create quite a buzz in the organization. For every employee who is a Machiavellian wannabe, there are thousands who conduct their daily worklives with integrity.

I have two issues with this chapter and they are to strongly convey the following:

1. Dirty politics are not a good long-term career strategy (though you may see them work occasionally over the short term).

2. People today are overly paranoid about dirty politics. Way too much energy is wasted thinking and acting defensively. The political maneuvering that people fear may be going on around them is probably not happening at all or is probably going to fizzle or become outdated before it can harm them. Organizations today are in a mode of constant change and days are filled with constant interruptions and detours.

HOW TO AVOID BEING THE VICTIM OF DIRTY TRICKS

◆ If something looks too good or too easy, there's probably something wrong with it. Scrutinize carefully.

◆ Beware of people who try to stress too much that they are doing you a favor. Beware of bullies, flatterers, and people who cut corners.

◆ Use caution if someone asks you to do something even a little unethical, like reneging on an agreement. This person may be just as unethical in his dealings with you.

◆ Don't be in too much of a hurry. Don't allow someone else's rush cause you to make a costly mistake. Keep a calm demeanor. Proceed as carefully as you need to.

◆ Take time to do all paperwork. Don't take shortcuts. There's usually a reason for all that paperwork. Someone learned the hard way that the paperwork was necessary. That's why we have contracts and clauses. Routine confirmations, follow-up calls, and paperwork can save costly and embarrassing mistakes—maybe your job.

◆ Question yourself if you begin to have to squeeze time, people, or resources to make something happen. Putting the squeeze on yourself, others, and schedules increases the opportunities for mistakes. If you feel you are forcing something, maybe the answer is that this event is not meant to be at this time. It's better to defer or reschedule and hope for a later opportunity to display your good work than to do shoddy work because you were under pressure and in a hurry.

The chart that follows will help give you an overview of the most popular underhanded maneuvers. Even better, the chart shows you tactics to combat the dirty tricks. You can effectively neutralize almost any dirty trick.

(**NOTE:** Use the How to Counter suggestions with caution. You must use your judgment before electing to use any of the tactics.)

DIRTY TRICK

1. Shoot down with torpedo comments. People with little or no talent love to shoot down the ideas and presentations of others. They make snide remarks, they challenge, they question. Sometimes, if they're really good at being bad, they can make their comments and questions sound innocent and genuine. After you put forth an idea, the attacker tries to torpedo you with a comment like one of these.

"Where are you going with this?"

"The real issue hasn't been solved," or "What's the point?"

"I'm confused."

"Do you know how much that would cost?"

"Have you any idea the labor that would take?"

"We haven't answered the larger question yet."

"Aren't we a little off track here?"

"Can you define that better?"

"Isn't that an exaggeration?"

"Are you sure?"

"I've never heard of such a thing."

"ACME Corporation has never done business like that."

"There are safety and security risks that you haven't even considered."

"You have some problems in this that need to be worked out."

"Haven't you forgotten something?"

"Looks shaky to me."

"Aren't there ethical implications?"

"That's a lot of work."

"That's fine in theory, but will it work?"

"What is this?"

"Whose idea *was* this?"

"Do you have research that backs this up?"

"Have you shown this to anyone in authority? in Engineering?"

"Just how long will all this take?"

"How does this compare to the success we had with X?"

"Has this been proven?"

HOW TO COUNTER

1. TACTICS

◆ Turn the question back on the attacker. If the attacker says, "What will happen to the staff if we do this?," answer, "What will happen in the long run if we don't?"

◆ Quietly, and with a very positive tone, ask the questioner to precisely and specifically spell out for you *exactly* what she means.

DIRTY TRICK

2. Tie the speaker up in knots by asking for specifics, measurable results, details:

"Where would we get that?" / "How would we do that?"

"How much return on investment (ROI) can we expect by year end?"

"Who's that?"

"Exactly how much fuel will that take over a year's time?"

"Will that happen half the time? Two thirds of the time?"

"What causes the ignition?"

"How many miles/pounds/ pork bellies is that?"

HOW TO COUNTER

2. TACTICS

◆ Say, "We are collaborating with you now to get you to tell us if this is a good idea. If you think so, we'll proceed with the details."

◆ "Our engineers/information specialists have that worked out. I leave that to them. If you'd like, I can bring one of them in to address the technical details."

◆ "We'll cover that in our next meeting. This meeting is to _____."

◆ "This is new to the company and to the industry. We're expecting great things. No one knows the precise amount yet, but it could be impressive."

DIRTY TRICK

3. Withhold information. One way to make sure you show up unprepared is for the trickster to delay giving you materials and information until the last minute. The trickster can tell your boss that she will pass on the info and then give it to you minutes before a meeting. You will have little time to prepare.

HOW TO COUNTER

3. TACTICS

◆ If you suspect materials are delayed, call the sender immediately. Now the trickster looks slipshod.

◆ Say, "The information John [the trickster] gave me this morning looks good. Before committing to such a serious task, I'd like to study it a bit more."

◆ The information looks good, but intriguing. I'd like to pursue a couple of things I saw in here, study them, then discuss them with you at length."

◆ I want to serve you in the best way I know how. Since I've had the documents for only two hours, I feel I want to study them more."

DIRTY TRICK

4. Assign an employee projects doomed to fail or that don't fit with his/her abilities. Firing someone is legally risky and requires lots of paperwork. One way to get rid of an employee easily is to assign him projects that he can't possibly complete successfully. A manager can assign an employee to find a method of disposing of fuel waste that is more cost-effective than the present method. If the manager knows that a recent study proved there is no more cost-effective method, then the employee's failure is guaranteed.

A variation of this dirty trick is to assign an employee tasks that don't suit his abilities. For example, if you know Bob is not a detail person and not neat and precise in recordkeeping, what do you do to get rid of him? Assign Bob to be the recordkeeper for a tediously detailed project. If you know Brenda is great in her area of expertise, but not a people person, you assign her to the front lines to develop new intra-departmental allies.

Some of this is acceptable as a developmental exercise, but if a manager consistently keeps Bob and Brenda away from tasks in which they could shine and puts them in situations guaranteed to fail, this is a dirty trick.

HOW TO COUNTER

4. TACTICS

◆ Document a memo to your boss. Thank him for his confidence in you. Tell him there are three points you would like to make.

◆ Document what your strengths are. Ask for projects that would allow you to put these strengths to work.

◆ Point out any concerns you have about the present project. Document any research that supports that this is not a viable project.

◆ Ask for an opportunity on the next project to do work more in line with your abilities. If you can't get out of this one, ask that your boss consider your request for a different sort of project next time. End with something like, "I want very much to make a contribution and ask for an opportunity to use my expertise for ACME Corporation."

◆ Make an appointment with your boss. Take the memo to the boss and discuss it in a friendly manner. Tell him you wrote your thoughts down because this was difficult for you to explain. Documentation threatens bosses.

DIRTY TRICK

5. Demeaning actions/comments disguised as helpfulness. Some conniving, condescending weasels can put you down while appearing to be very helpful. They fuss around your project fixing this, adjusting that, offering you last-minute advice on something you did not do quite right. They will even subtly criticize you by doing little things.

◆ Picking lint or a thread off your jacket, adjusting your collar, or saying, "Did you know your hem hangs lower in the back?" Pick. Pick. Pick. Like Chinese water torture this can wear away self-confidence. If you don't handle this right, you'll look stupid.

◆ Adjusting, aligning, or fixing up charts, graphics, presentation. The message is, "This project is so shoddy. It would go to hell in a handbasket if it weren't for my rescuing it."

◆ Coming in at the last minute and adding content that is superficial, then taking a lion's share of the credit. These corporate thieves even go surreptitiously to your boss and say, "The project is okay now. I went in there and filled in what was needed."

HOW TO COUNTER

5. TACTICS

◆ Hide out. If you know a person is a critic or a credit stealer, go to a conference room on another floor to finish up or telecommute (with your boss's permission.) Whatever you do, steer clear of these glory hogs.

◆ If you're ambushed and must deal with these folks:

◆ Give in, but limit the nitpicker's scope. Tell him you want to do the other parts of the project yourself, but that he can really help if he will polish up *one* section, or do the graphics. Send him away with busy work and complete your project in peace.

◆ Be honest. Say, "Every project has last-minute improvements that could make it perfect. I find, however, that I do better if I relax and focus just before a presentation instead of worrying with the details. At this point, I'm going with it the way it is. I need this time to concentrate on more important issues."

◆ Consider accepting his help gratefully. Sometimes our critics do us great favors by pointing out flaws our friends would never tell us. If you can manage it, this might be your best tactic. Consider it to be the equivalent to hiring a consultant to come in to bulletproof your project.

◆ To help derail the trickster in his attempt to steal your credit, try this dirty trick of your own. In front of your boss and/or others, thank the trickster for one *very* small, insignificant thing he did: "Thank you for your positive feedback on the project. And Arthur, thank you for doing the bibliography for me. That was a big help." Anything Arthur says about the other work he did will sound petty. You look magnanimous. Arthur has been put in his place.

◆ Do the same tactics to him the next time. At the close of his project, do all the tweaking, lint picking, credit stealing behaviors that he did.

DIRTY TRICK

6. Keep changing the agenda, presentation, or plan. Leave one employee out of the loop. She'll look unprepared. If you're caught, you can say you thought everyone had been informed. This can actually look like an honest mistake on the trickster's part. Or, the victim's honesty might be questioned as to whether she actually received the changes and has created an alibi.

HOW TO COUNTER

6. TACTICS

Take your medicine and keep quiet—*today*. Tomorrow, go to your boss with a proactive plan. Say something like, "I want to make sure that what happened yesterday never happens again. We fumbled through yesterday, but a mistake like that could cost us a client/a lot of money/etc. Because I was left out of the loop of information, our presentation was not as professional as it could be. That's in the past. Going forward, I have a solution."

◆ Your solution could be to establish an e-mail forwarding list for project updates: a five-minute conference call the day before presentation, or circulating a sheet for participants to list changes.

◆ Don't look resentful. Look professional and proactive.

◆ Document

DIRTY TRICK

7. When an employee confronts a trickster, the trickster may make the victim look bad by saying:

"You are paranoid. I just forgot. Everyone makes mistakes."

"You have a problem."

"If you think I did that on purpose, you're crazy."

"Get a life."

"You only want to talk about this one thing. Everyone's tired of your harping on it. You can't acknowledge how well XYZ (another project) is going. What are you, jealous?"

"I'm only human."

"You make mistakes, too."

HOW TO COUNTER

7. TACTICS

◆ This is not a good time to have this discussion. Say, "Clearly you're upset. Let's set aside some time to find some positive solutions. I'm only interested in making our future projects a success. What time tomorrow is good for you?"

◆ Don't meet with the trickster alone. Try to get your boss to meet with you. Try to have an ally in the meeting. Before the meeting, go to the boss or ally. Stress that you are having trouble getting the trickster to stick to the issues and work on solutions. Ask for help in keeping the meeting proactive and focused on productivity. Remind them what's at stake: money, production, rework, customer service.

DIRTY TRICK

8. Letter of the law or malicious compliance is a popular trick.
You ask your secretary to help set up for a meeting for 30 people. You tell her that you'll need 30 chairs and 5 tables. Later, you tell her that only the department chairmen will meet. That's only 5 people. She makes you look ridiculous by having a huge room set up.

She says, "You said 30 chairs and 5 tables, and that's what you got."

She holds you responsible for not spelling out for her that only 5 chairs were needed after the change.

HOW TO COUNTER

8. TACTICS

◆ Ask the trickster what she thinks a solution could be.

◆ If the trickster reports to you, put innovation and initiative as part of her developmental goals.

◆ If the person is a peer, ask the boss to give the group training in initiative, innovation, and problem solving.

◆ Ask for team goals for cooperation. Get others invested in making you a success.

DIRTY TRICK

9. Telling people what to do is a way to look large and in charge. If the trickster sees Bill starting to reorganize the warehouse, he wanders over and says loudly in front of the boss, "Bob, I think we should reorganize this warehouse." Or he sees Bill checking costs of trash pickup and finding new vendors, and says, "Bill, I think we should explore other vendors for trash pickup. That's my plan for reducing costs."

HOW TO COUNTER

9. TACTICS

Say something like, "That project started two days ago. Didn't I tell you?"

or

"My staff has been looking into that for some time. Our final report is in the making."

or

"Where have you been? That's old news. The decision is almost made."

DIRTY TRICK

10. Voice a lot of platitudes. Make it sound as if the victim doesn't agree with these wise and good attitudes.

"I realize not everyone agrees, but I believe we have to go outside the scope of our jobs sometimes to help."

"To me, serving the customer is what's important."

"Call me crazy, but I think accuracy is still important in our industry."

"I don't believe in wasting time or money, even if they're not mine."

"I feel I owe a day's work for a day's pay."

HOW TO COUNTER

10. TACTICS

◆ Agree. Say, "That's why we work so well together. We share the same values."

or

◆ "I've never worked with anyone on this staff who didn't believe that."

◆ After agreeing, add a platitude of your own: "I believe in a day's work for a day's pay, but to succeed we sometimes have to go that extra mile."

DIRTY TRICK

11. Dirty tricksters create a smokescreen of good deeds to hide their evil doings. They make a great show of helping old ladies cross the street, working for abused children, and other saintly deeds to throw management off the scent of their foul deeds.

They also create a few loyal fans in strategic positions. These fans have known them for years and have never seen them do one underhanded thing. That's because a dirty trickster is sneaky. The trickster is good, kind, helpful, and scrupulous in all dealings with key people—particularly the boss. It's a great strategy because when you accuse the trickster of dishonesty or incompetence, the trickster has greater credibility than you do.

Tricksters choose to play up to people that other employees think are saints. You see, if the sainted employee thinks the trickster is virtuous, then everyone assumes that's correct.

HOW TO COUNTER

11. TACTICS

◆ Try to set up other people to "discover" the trickster's evil deeds. You may tarnish your own credibility by accusations. Remember that the trickster is very slick. He may have a plan for pinning the blame on you. In some cases you have to ignore the problem.

◆ Keep your ears open. The trickster has done these things to someone else before you. Let them come to you; don't seek them out. Let them do 99 percent of the talking. Your role is only to be a good listener—very responsive.

◆ Ask open questions. The other person may eventually speak up instead of you. That's ideal.

ACTION ITEMS

1. Are there any dirty tricks going on in your department currently? If so, list two things you should do to counter these tactics.

   _____

   _____

2. Think back to a time that a coworker used dirty tricks to make
   life difficult for you. Which of the tactics in this chapter could
   you have used?

   _____

   _____

Chapter 6

◆

Building Your Power: Networking and Publicizing Your Accomplishments

It is better to be looked over than overlooked.

—Mae West

Skill, talent, and experience are highly overrated; success in mid-size to large companies is much more related to your networking and public relations efforts. Surveys often rank what you know and how qualified you are as Number 5 or 6 on the list of indicators of career success. One extensive survey of sales professionals ranked product knowledge number 12!

> It's not what you know; it's whom you know and, more importantly, who knows you that determine career success.

Networking
Start today to build a network of people who will help promote you, market you, and help you secure both jobs and recognition.

Networking Strategies
1. Join at least one and preferably two professional organizations. One should relate to your industry or field; the other should be a leadership or management society that will give you exposure to other industries in case your industry goes through lean times.

   Joining professional organizations is by far the best career strategy I know for leapfrogging to better positions and pay. Why?

   ◆ People you meet in professional organizations are in a better position to hire you or recommend you than other groups.

◆ You will hear about more good job opportunities.

◆ You will have an "in" when you apply for a position you have heard about through a professional organization. You will also be there first, before the hordes of applicants send in résumés. Many good jobs never hit the classifieds. Headhunters handle them. Friends help friends scoop the good jobs.

◆ Your skills and sophistication will be constantly updated. That increases job security.

◆ You will meet the top people in your field.

◆ Employers and prospective employers are more impressed by your credentials if you are a member of a professional organization. This is totally illogical since almost anyone can write a dues check and join. Still, membership says to some people that you are continuing to update and polish your professional skills—whether it's true or not.

Here are some scary thoughts:

– The accountant who botched more taxes than anyone I know was president of our local CPA society. He is incompetent as an accountant, but he is a great volunteer and faithful club member. He has a thriving practice that attracts new clients in droves because his credentials look so impressive.

– The least talented speaker I know was once president of our professional speaker's organization.

You see, being president of the local Human Resources society doesn't require that you be a great Human Resources professional; it only requires that you pay your dues, run for office, and volunteer your time. Still, when you list that you are the president of such an organization on your résumé, the job market places a higher value on you. Even your current boss may have more respect for you.

2. Once a week, call or write to someone you don't know or don't know well and acknowledge her for something she did well.

◆ Read your company newsletter and compliment the Toys for Tots volunteer coordinator for collecting over 300 toys.

◆ Watch an interview with a senior vice president on your company's closed circuit television network. Drop a note saying how much you appreciated her explanation of how the futures market is affecting the company's stock price.

◆ Call the manager of Information Resources and tell him how much better the new e-mail system is. Thank him for making the decision to switch.

◆ You see someone's name in the paper you haven't heard from in a while. Perhaps the article simply says that this person is a volunteer for the Can Drive to Stamp Out Hunger. Call her and say how great it is that she's making this contribution to the community.

3. Join a networking group. Some groups meet for the sole purpose of networking. They may meet once a month for breakfast or quarterly for cocktails. This networking is blatant and energetic. Cards are exchanged constantly and people market their services and companies.

Most great connections we make in our careers come from unlikely sources. Someone who knows someone who knows us tells us about a great opportunity or gets us an interview. We rarely get our big break from the people we thought would be our most influential allies. It's important to let everyone know what you do and that you're successful at it. That way, when they hear of your dream job, they will know to contact you. Some of these sources are

◆ spouses of coworkers
◆ church friends
◆ parents at children's athletic events and school
◆ neighbors
◆ secretaries and clerical people (often, they hear a lot!)

Practice a short, crisp reply to people who ask what you do. Simply say that you design on-line training for adults. Don't go into detail about topics. If they're interested, they'll ask.

4. Leave your business card everywhere. If you drop by to see someone and she's out, leave your business card. Even if you write a personal note to leave behind, jot it on your card. Your card with your name and what you do printed on it is very effective at increasing your visibility.

If you leave some copies of your neighborhood newsletter on your neighbor's doorstep, leave your card, also.

5. Donate to local school and charitable auctions. It's great free advertising to a select group of highly influential people. Donate books related to your profession or gift certificates for free services. Your gift is usually printed up in a catalog or displayed at a fund-raiser. Lots of people see a brief description of your company and your services along with your gift. These people are the movers and shakers in your community.

You can donate a meal at a fine restaurant, a print, a job tool, a service, or something related to your profession.

6. The next time you are putting together a group to go to lunch or out for a run after work, add one person to the group who's outside your usual sphere. Branch out. Get to know more people who can help you.

7. Ask more than one person to mentor you. Your company may assign you a mentor. That doesn't mean you can't ask additional people to unofficially mentor you. The more people you get invested in your career success, the better.

8. Attend every company function possible. If Information Resources is launching a new service at a meeting in the cafeteria for their employees, ask an Information Resource employee if you can attend. Talking about how cool the new service is can be a great way to network with a different group outside your department.

9. When a coworker mentions a respected peer or a higher-level manager they happen to know, ask for an introduction. Say, "He sounds like a great guy. Maybe the next time he comes by your office you could let me know. I'd like to meet him."

10. Network with people from your past, present, and future. Keeping up the ties you have already established is as important as making connections for the future. To maintain strong ties:

    ◆ Once a year, call a couple of people from your former company. Ask about their lives and issues.
    ◆ Call former mentors, managers, and other advocates each time you get promoted or change jobs.
    ◆ Keep in touch, at least annually, with people in other departments in which you once worked.

11. Write Christmas or Hanukkah cards. Better yet, write Thanksgiving or St. Patrick's Day cards. Choose a holiday and send cards to everyone you know or have ever known. People appreciate these cards, now more than ever. Include a very brief newsy update of your life, preferably handwritten.

12. Join your company's Toastmaster's Club. This is a great way to build relationships in other departments while polishing your presentation skills. If your company has no Toastmaster's group, start one! You will be viewed as a mover and a shaker.

13. Attend company events that will give you exposure: an executive's speech in the lobby, presentations, the company picnic, fund-raisers, and races sponsored by your company or vendors or customers, and anything else that will give you positive exposure.

Blow Your Own Horn
Listed below are some of the most destructive myths for career-minded people.

◆ If you do a good job, people will notice—NOT!

- ◆ Management knows who's the real talent and brains of a project—NOT!
- ◆ Long hours and hard work will be rewarded—NOT!
- ◆ Don't blow your own horn / Never vote for yourself / Be modest about your accomplishments—NOT! NOT! NOT!

If you have been in the workplace for any length of time, you know that people who blow their own horn are usually the ones rewarded. These cagey folks have learned the art of self-promotion. If they happen to have brains and are hard workers, that's a great combination.

We all know people, however, who are the first ones to work and the last ones to leave. They're quiet, and dependable, but no one views them as the stars of tomorrow. We also know people with little substance, no brilliant ideas, and not particularly hardworking, who seem tapped for the fast track for no reason other than that they've convinced the brass that they're the greatest. First and foremost, these talented egoists *believe* they're the greatest. This effusive self-confidence is contagious. Others around them catch it and gain confidence in these up-and-comers, whether that confidence is merited or not.

Here are some ways to make others perceive you as the heir apparent to the next great job.

1. Keep a file handy that lists the addresses of your local newspaper, the e-mail address of your company newsletter, newspaper, and/or magazine, the e-mail addresses of publications by professional organizations, neighborhood newsletters, and other media that touch your life. Have several 5 × 7 black-and-white glossy pictures of yourself in the file, also.

Whenever you are named head of a committee or get promoted, you will have the addresses and picture ready to legitimately broadcast the good news that you are climbing yet another rung on the ladder of success. People often assume that someone else is reporting the details of your good news, so it isn't perceived as bragging.

E-mail submissions are great, if the publication accepts them. You can simply forward the news item to a long list of recipients.

Note: If you live in a small town or suburb, be sure to send the item to the big-city newspaper near you as well as to your local paper. For really big moves in corporate circles, contact the *Wall Street Journal* and *USA Today* and your field's leading trade journal.

2. By far the most successful PR tool is the grapevine. In a humble way, share how fortunate you feel to be given the opportunity to serve as the United Way Chairperson or work for Doug Brandt, Director of Operations. For more tips for using the grapevine, which studies show to be 83 to 95 percent effective, see Chapter 1, Career Move number 7.

3. Prompt your boss or others to announce your success in meetings or at other events. How do you do this without appearing to be a self-serving jerk? One way is to ask your boss to tout the event, but don't mention yourself. When your boss stands up and promotes the event, she most likely will mention your role.

Examples:

◆ Ask your boss if she will announce that the United Way Drive is underway and ask for everyone's support. In all probability, she will remember to tell them that you have been chosen chairperson.

◆ Ask your boss to mention that you're hiring sales engineers and that the current sales staff is receiving an incentive bonus for submitting names of qualified candidates. Your boss might also mention that the hiring is for a new department just created to handle high-tech companies and that you've been named to head it up.

4. Don't limit your PR to promotions and job changes. Try to get media exposure for any effort or recognition.

◆ launching a new product
◆ major hiring effort—adding new jobs to the community
◆ moving into a new office
◆ regional recognition for sales, productivity, quality
◆ five-year, ten-year, fifteen-year anniversaries of joining a company
◆ becoming certified in anything
◆ volunteer activities, such as becoming the soccer coach of your daughter's team, becoming the refreshment stand volunteer coordinator, heading the pool committee for your neighborhood, becoming a Welcome Wagon representative, winning your company's speaking contest, hosting a dignitary or important businessperson from out of town, hosting a meeting of volunteers at your home, and taking time to tour a sister company while you are on your vacation in another country

5. Sponsor athletic teams, put ads in student newspapers, or pay for the printing of programs for school or cultural events. Be sure recognition is given for these things. School, cultural, and athletic groups are always asking for sponsorship in various ways. This is a great way to promote name recognition. Put an ad in the Little League Program that says, "Go, Tigers!" Sign it "Doug Jones, CPA."

6. Volunteer to print up the program for the school play and make sure this is printed at the bottom of the first page: "Printing Provided by Doug Jones, CPA." Make sure as many people as possible know who you are and what you do.

Wayne Paulsen, a local attorney, just landed a huge multimillion-dollar account this way. His law firm is located in a small southern suburb. His new account is a major bank headquartered in the Pacific Northwest. How did Wayne find this plum client? He didn't. They found him.

Here's how it went. The president of the northwestern bank's biological father had lived in the same southern suburb as

Wayne. The bank president had been brought up by his mother and stepfather in Seattle and had no ties or contacts in the South. When the banker's father died without a will, however, the banker needed someone he could trust to handle probate locally. The banker called an old college buddy in Wayne's community. The college buddy's daughter played soccer with Wayne's daughter. The college buddy knew Wayne was an attorney because Wayne purchased the jerseys for the team and had his law firm's name printed on the back of the shirts.

The estate was in a mess. Wayne handled everything with patience and efficiency. He looked for opportunities to save on fees and taxes. At the end, the bank president was very grateful. He asked Wayne to handle any legal business the bank had in the Southeast. As it turned out, that amounted to over $100,000 a year in legal fees!

This is another example of the strength of weak ties. Most big breaks people get come from some of the most unexpected sources. Be sure people know your name in case they have an unexpected reason to contact you.

7. Join your company's speaker's bureau. If schools or civic groups in the community occasionally ask your company for speakers, volunteer to speak. You get to know lots of people this way. More important, they get to know you. All the practice you will receive as a speaker will hone your skills for when you make the all-important company speeches.

8. Develop your own 20-minute talk to deliver to civic groups and other organizations. People are always looking for speakers for breakfasts, lunches, monthly meetings, and conferences. You can perfect an entertaining twenty-minute talk that will showcase you as an expert. Here are typical topic areas of interest.

- local history
- saving money
- retirement / taxes
- humor
- new technology
- editorials (see this style on newspaper editorial page)

9. For great PR inside your company, do a variation of number 8. Choose a topic of interest to people in your company. Suggestions:

- industry trends
- new technology
- a new product or service
- an area of professional development
- leadership
- motivation
- communication

Develop a 20-minute talk. Next, e-mail all the managers in your company that you are available to do your presentation at staff meetings. Be sure to clear this first with your boss. Position this as part of your professional development.

Note: Be sure you practice your presentation to perfection before you present it. This is supposed to be positive PR; it could backfire if you appear unprofessional. Also, remember that people today expect speakers to be entertaining. Have an interactive or humorous part of your talk to bring it alive. Demonstrations are also popular.

In short, make sure your name is presented often and always in a positive light. Be creative in inventing new ways to promote your career. You can become an industry legend. Start the legend yourself.

ACTION ITEMS

List five steps you will take in the next 90 days to network or publicize your accomplishments:

1. _____

2. _____

3. _____

4. _____

5. _____

Chapter 7

---◆---

Major Players in Your Company and How to Get Them to Go to Bat for You

Tell me thy company, and I'll tell thee what thou art.

—Cervantes
Don Quixote (1605–15)

WHO ARE YOUR ALLIES?

So many people in your company can give your career a boost, a helping hand, a shove in the right direction. How do you motivate them to do these things for you?

First of all, you need to identify the people in your company who could be valuable allies. Only you can know who is influential in your organization. Here is my list. You can add to it based on what you know about your corporate culture.

◆ Human Resources manager
◆ recruitment professionals
◆ organizational development professionals
◆ executive V.P.s and above
◆ heads, assistants, and top secretaries in departments in which you would like to work
◆ recognized movers and shakers and stars
◆ vice president of your functional area
◆ public relations professionals/manager
◆ training director

STRATEGIC PLAN FOR DEVELOPING POWERFUL ALLIES

The following plan lists each major player, why he or she is important to your career, and strategies for winning support. Of course, all the strategies for coworkers and bosses (Chapters 3 and 9) will work for these politicos, too. The moves below are in addition to what you have already learned.

1. Human Resources Manager, Talent Management, Employees and Recruitment Professionals

Importance: Can give you a heads up when plum jobs in other areas are opening up. Being there first is a huge advantage in a recruitment search. Some jobs are never advertised or posted because the right person was connected with the hiring manager and was quickly and quietly placed.

Human Resources people also sometimes have the power to enhance a salary range, raise a job to a higher level, or throw in benefits or moving expenses. You never know when you'll need a little help, but when you do, the help is extremely valuable. If your job is rated at a higher level, the increase in pay will benefit you every day for years. Don't underestimate the value of these professionals.

STRATEGIES FOR WINNING THIS ALLY

◆ If your company has difficulty filling certain positions, help them. Offer to post the jobs in your church's help wanted directory. If the job is similar to yours, offer to advertise or make announcements in the newsletter of your professional organization(s).

◆ If Human Resources has a large Saturday event like a job fair, offer to man a booth, hand out applications, or bring donuts to the staff for a break. Make sure this does not interfere with your job.

◆ Thank these professionals for what they do. Acknowledge a good hire they made. On your one-, five-, or ten-year anniversary, send a thank-you note to the person who hired you. Commend him on recognizing a good fit.

◆ Is there a new employee orientation? Offer to help (if that's okay with your boss). This is also a good way to network with new employees.

2. Organizational Development Professionals

Importance: They design the plans for mergers, downsizings, layoffs, and other major corporate upheavals. They decide who goes where. They decide whose jobs go away. O.D. (or O.E. for Organizational Effectiveness) people can determine your corporate future or your lack of one within your present organization. They may also be able to help you move into a viable part of the organization if your department gets the axe.

STRATEGIES FOR WINNING THIS ALLY

◆ O.D. people usually form lots of focus groups and committees. Volunteer to serve. That way, you'll be in the know early about what's going on in the company. You must have a plausible reason for volunteering. Try one of these.

– My industrial management professor in college got me interested in O.D. Please call on me if you need volunteers for focus groups or other committees.

– A good friend of mine works in O.D. at General Motors. He says it's hard to find committed volunteers for focus groups. I'd be happy to serve if you need me.

◆ Be open to change. By the time an organizational consultant comes to you with a reorganization plan, it's pretty much a done deal. The top brass has decided how things are going to be. You might as well embrace it, support it, be its loudest cheerleader. If not, you are "not on board with the way we do things now." Even if you are right in your criticisms, you'll probably be fired.

◆ Once a year, call O.D. and ask if there are any skills you, as a manager, should be working with your people to develop. Say, "From an O.D. (or O.E.) standpoint, what should I be investing my time in to help prepare my department for the future?" Then, let them talk. Don't offer many, if any, opinions.

3. Executive V.P.s and Above

Importance: The Japanese know the importance of having senior people mentor and sponsor these much lower in the hierarchy. In fact, their mentors are at least two levels higher than the person they mentor. Don't be aggressive in pursuing executive level support, but don't be invisible to them either.

STRATEGIES FOR WINNING THIS ALLY

◆ Read the business section of the paper, the local news, or your company's newsletter and magazines for the mention of executive names. These articles usually recognize an accomplishment: promoted, named to a committee, hosting an event, or an award. Write a simple note on plain, good-quality white or cream notecard stationery. Say something like this:

Dear Mr. Boren,

Congratulations on being named Group Vice President. I am just one of many employees at ACME Corporation who wishes you well.

Sincerely,

John Doe
Engineer I
Power Delivery Division

Don't gush or flatter too much—that's too obvious.

If you have worked with this executive before, you should throw in a line about that:
From watching you in action on the United Way Campaign, I know you will bring great energy to this leadership position.

◆ Do volunteer work in the charities these executives sponsor. Volunteer work is the great equalizer of different levels in the corporate hierarchy. You rub shoulders in a volunteer project with corporate superstars that you might never run into at the office.

Also, if you excel, you get recognition that carries over into the workplace. If you secure more corporate sponsors than anyone for the charitable golf tournament a V.P. is chairing, then you become known as a go-getter. If you contribute more sweat equity than anyone else to the Habitat for Humanity House your company is building, the executive in charge will see that you are a hard worker. She will probably also see you and come to recognize you at work. That can only enhance your status.

4. **Heads, assistants, and top secretaries in departments in which you would like to work**

   Importance: In which department would you most like to work? Set as a goal gaining entry into that department. The more allies you have there, the sooner you'll be likely to win a position there. If there's lots of good buzz about you in a department, something will open up eventually. Often, a secretary can be as influential as a vice president in getting you an interview. Figure out who the key influencers are. Then proceed to make allies of them.

STRATEGIES FOR WINNING THIS ALLY

◆ If this department serves your department or vice versa, include their secretaries in your Secretaries Day Luncheon or other training events or anything that's considered a perk. Tell them it's because you appreciate them.

◆ Set up a meeting annually with these contacts if they serve you or vice versa. If you serve them, the meeting's purpose is to ask what you can do even better next year to serve them than in the past. Thank them for their cooperation.

If they serve you, the meeting is to acknowledge the things they have done right. Explain that problems come up and are discussed as they occur throughout the year. This brief meeting is to acknowledge their strengths: meeting deadlines, reliability, fewer errors, friendly customer service, integrity, attractive packaging, expertise, etc.

5. Recognized movers, shakers, and stars

Importance: Hang out with a star and catch some of their glow. Be known as one of an elite group that will one day run the company. If one of the stars of tomorrow has time to chat with you, maybe management will feel they should take you more seriously. Plus, these people may really be running the company one day. You want to be one of their senior executives or maybe their heir to the throne.

STRATEGIES FOR WINNING THIS ALLY

- ◆ Most stars have huge egos. Play up to that. Send notes of congratulations for every accomplishment. Give them a thumbs-up or an "attaboy" in the hallway.
- ◆ Call them and ask for career advice, if you think that's not too aggressive. Tell them that you admire how they have managed their career. Ask if they have 30 minutes to spend with you, discussing how they have risen so fast so soon.
- ◆ Ask the star to speak at your Kiwanis or other civic club. Ask her to speak about something in her field of expertise or about success or leadership. Tell her that she is a role model for many people like you and that you feel that you and others could learn a lot from her.

If not too risky, try the outrageous technique of being absolutely honest. Tell the star something like this.

Susan, one day, I believe you will be running this company. When you do, I want to work for you. If you see any projects or events that we can work together on in the meantime, please call on me. You can count on my full support.

6. Vice president of your functional area

Importance: He can lend you support now, even if your boss doesn't see your worth. He can make your boss think twice before he does something you won't like. He can see you as a candidate for a better job in another area, even if your boss can't see it.

STRATEGIES FOR WINNING THIS ALLY

◆ Send an e-mail once or twice a year on a topic that is considered to be the V.P.'s areas of expertise. (Don't do this if you have a boss who wants *nothing* to go above her head that she doesn't authorize.) The V.P. of Human Resources might specialize in corporate culture surveys. Send him an article about a new type of corporate culture survey. The V.P. of Marketing might be an expert in vertical marketing. Send an article on that, with only a line or two of your own added. Sign your name, position, and department.

◆ Participate in any department or division-wide event, fundraiser, competition, newsletter, etc. Make sure your name comes up—a lot. Attend every Christmas party, product announcement, and company picnic. These are good opportunities to just say "Hello" and introduce yourself. If volunteers are needed to serve food or emcee games, be there front and center.

◆ Look for ways to save the department money—even small ways. At the end of the year, create a one-page chart showing the savings you have accomplished. Send this to your boss. She will probably pass this on to the top since it makes her look good, too. Make sure your name and your boss's name are visible, as in this example.

ANNUALIZED SAVINGS

Submitted to: <u>your boss's name here</u>

Developed by: <u>your name here</u>

Co-generation Department		
Savings Opportunity	**Amount of Savings**	**Annualized Savings**
Reuse Paper for Daily Reports	$5.00 daily	$1,075.00
Change of Old Lighting Fixtures	$180 month (net after investment)	$2,160.00
1x Daily Reporting of Trucks Instead of 2x	$18 hour per driver × <u>1.5</u> hour each $27.00 × <u>30</u> drivers $810 daily	$174,150.00
Recycling Paper Savings on Waste: Services Savings on Paper	$220/month $100/month	$3,840.00
TOTAL		$181,225.00

◆ Create a bulletin board or suggest that the department create a bulletin board to recognize employee accomplishments. Be sure to get your picture, your clippings, and your name posted up there often. *Advertising pays.* (It can be an electronic bulletin board or web site or via e-mail.)

◆ Find out if your company has a mentoring program. Ask to be mentored by this executive. You may get turned down, but the executive may be flattered that you requested him.

7. Public relations professions / manager

Importance: Can get your name in front of the right people in a positive light. Because they interface with all departments, these pros can put out some good buzz about you.

STRATEGIES FOR WINNING THIS ALLY

These folks need you as much as you need them. They often have to beat the bushes for positive PR to tell others about what the company and its employees are doing.

Throughout the year, type up very brief paragraphs telling about positive things you participated in. For example, here are some headlines for typical newsworthy items.

◆ Karen Green Leads Team to Collect Highest Amount Ever for United Way
◆ Karen Green Named Assistant to Vice President Kelley
◆ Karen Green Elected to School Board
◆ Corporate Climate Survey Successfully Completed by Group Led by Karen Green
◆ Audit Team Meets IRS Challenge, Led by Karen Green
◆ New Committee to Study Recycling; Karen Green Named Chair

8. Training directors

Importance: These folks talk to everyone. They are great people to network with. Because they deal with improving the professionalism of others, training experts are credible references when they praise your professionalism. They know a little about what's going on in every part of the company. In particular, they know what the needs are. They can advise you on job opportunities and what the hot topics are in every area.

STRATEGIES FOR WINNING THIS ALLY

◆ Attend every training class possible. Participate, participate, participate. Be sure you get your prework in on time. Don't complain about the food or facilities. Praise the internal training department.
◆ Call the training director. Say how much you have enjoyed the high-caliber training offered. Mention a couple of specific courses. Then volunteer to be a student in any pilots. A pilot is a new course or a course in the process of being designed.

You often get to work with the training brass in a pilot. Demonstrate your intelligence, your team approach, and your good judgment. Don't monopolize but do participate.

◆ If your training department doesn't provide snacks at coffee break, bring some in on the last day of training. Stop by a grocery store and pick up doughnuts, muffins, and fruit. You will be remembered fondly.

◆ Send a thank-you note or e-mail to the instructor and training director after every course.

◆ If you have an interview with another functional area, call a training director or instructor with whom you have rapport. Ask if he can advise you about topics of interest to the decision maker or problem areas to stay away from.

◆ Help the instructor set up tables or clean up the room at the end of the day. Often tables need to be moved or items need to be carried to storage. Early morning setup time and late afternoon cleanup times are great times for one-on-one conversations. The instructor is very busy, however, so keep conversations brief and light.

◆ Attempt to have a casual, "Oh, by the way" conversation with a trainer or training manager. Say that although you have been pleased with your development in your present area, you believe you need exposure to other parts of the company. Ask where he sees areas of opportunity around the company. Ask who the decision makers are.

ACTION ITEMS

1. Spend an hour studying your company. Pinpoint two or three people who could potentially help your career. Be sure to choose at least one person in a totally different area of the company from the one in which you work. List their names on the chart below.

2. Fill out the first two or three lines on the chart below.

I. Name of ally	II. Short- or long-term ally	III. When was your most recent contact?	IV. What could you do to support this person?
Example: John Doe	short-term	May 2000	A. Send thank-you note for services B. Volunteer to help with survey C.
1.			A. B. C.
2.			A. B. C.
3.			A. B. C.
4.			A. B. C.

3. Look at ally number 1 above. Choose an item from this ally's column IV. (either A, B, or C.) Do one of these tasks this week.
4. Do the same for ally number 2 as you did for number 1.
5. Look at your list of allies. Is there anyone with whom you feel comfortable discussing your career goals at this time? If so, make an appointment. Tell him your goals. Ask for his help. If now is not a good time for any of these allies, do this in a month or two. Within three months, you must ask at least one ally for help. The more you ask, the more you get. Asking for help is awkward, but to advance you must do it. Some allies may not help. If you ask enough people, eventually you'll find an ally who is in a position to advance your career.

Chapter 8

Beginning or Exiting a Job: Opportunity for Bridge Building or Disaster

Every exit is an entry somewhere else.

—Tom Stoppard

Beginning a New Job

Imagine this:

You are standing on a steep precipice overlooking a gorge far deeper than the Grand Canyon. You are on the very edge of a little rock shelf that juts out gamely over the giant pit below.

You have been given special powers that can be used only on this precipice at this time and then those powers will never be given to you again. If you use the power correctly, you will be given the gift of flight. You will be able to soar above the pit, mount higher than you've ever gone before, and experience the joy of flight. If you don't use the powers correctly, you will fall like a rock into the pit and be destroyed.

That's pretty much the opportunity you have when you begin a new job—the opportunity to soar to new heights or to fall into oblivion or disrepute. Cheerful thought, huh?

The analogy is apt in another way, also. You have some exceptional strategic opportunities to influence people and politics when you begin a job. Some opportunities, like the ones that follow, will never come again. This is your chance to

◆ influence your coworkers' and your boss's perception of you.
◆ create an instant reputation for being hardworking, brilliant, a team player, creative, cautious, neat, or any attribute.
◆ create an instant reputation for the opposite of those traits.
◆ leave an indelible picture of what your professional image is. People will categorize you.
◆ set boundaries for what you will do and won't do, what you will accept and won't accept. This can range from asking people not to smoke in your office to telling your boss that you don't see your role as doing certain administrative tasks.
◆ impress the socks off people. No matter how good you are, it's difficult to impress people who work around us every day. If you ever want to be viewed as an impressive person, this is the time to quietly and sensitively reveal the full power of your intellect and accomplishments. You cannot walk up to a coworker six months from now and say, "I was once awarded a National Endowment for the Humanities Fellowship at Stanford University." Out of the blue, that's bragging. Also, the coworker may think you're living in the past.

It's perfectly acceptable, however, to drop facts like these on people during interviews or in some introductions. If your boss is going to introduce you at a staff meeting, give her a short list (three or four) of the things you'd like her to include. You can also highlight these on your résumé for her before she introduces you or passes the résumé on to others.

◆ tell your boss what you really think. You can plead ignorance and question how things are done better now than later. If you see a terribly inefficient way something is done, you may be able to ask your boss with wide-eyed innocence about why it's done that way. In later months, your questioning will be a bad political move and seem critical or second guessing.

◆ meet upper management. Your boss may take you "upstairs" to meet executives. Make the best use of this exposure. Be informed about what else this executive manages before you meet her. Ask your boss to tell you a little about the executive ahead of time. Don't talk too much but drop at least one tidbit into the conversation that makes you look current, innovative, and intelligent. If branding is a hot issue at your new company, try to work in a comment about the good examples of branding you've seen from her department. Link something she says to what's going on in the stock market this week to show you are a student of the business. The comment should be short and tied to something she said first. Don't just spout neat stuff to impress.

Also, try to have a good question prepared. The question should not put the executive on the spot or appear challenging or aggressive.

◆ meet people in other departments and let them know about your skills and experience. The best internal job hunting you will ever do is at the beginning of this job. Make other departments wish they'd seen you first. They will remember you when that next job opens up and try to steal you away. Consider these first week introductions as a showcase to market yourself for your next move upward.

◆ make possible future enemies look bad. If they go after the new guy, they look bad. Draw their dirty tricks into the open. Again, go to your boss in wide-eyed innocence and ask questions that will bust your evil coworker for messing with you. For example, ask your boss, "Danny told me the department's tradition is that the new hire always opens the reception area and starts the coffee in the morning. What do I do Friday when I go to have my fingerprints made? Do I get the last person hired before me to cover?"

Your boss needs to know what's going on but you can't complain—not yet.

◆ set standards for yourself and disclose any beliefs that might affect your working relationship. Without spending a lot of time talking about yourself, you can cheerfully let people know if their humor, biases, habits, or conversation are in any way offensive to you. With a light touch say something like the following:

> You may as well know, I run a G-rated cubicle.

> I'm going to ask the waitress to separate the checks. I'd feel better not putting this on my expense report.

> Don't preach, just state succinctly what you will do or won't do.

Starting a New Job: Ten Strategic Moves

When your boss extends the offer to you to join the company, you may be in a position to ask for some things. If you feel that the boss really wants you, your input, and ideas, consider asking for one or more of the following:

1. Ask to meet the key people in other departments you will be interfacing with in the future. Do this on the premise that you will work more productively with them this way. Keep in mind that you are simultaneously marketing yourself to rise in the company by being hired away by these other departments.

2. Create a wish list for your boss. Tell her that since your first interview you have allowed yourself to do some brainstorming and idea generating about what you'd eventually like to do if the sky were the limit. Be sure to say that you realize that all these expenditures won't be possible, but that you hope some will be doable. Be very sure that you are dealing with a boss who is willing to spend money. Again, be very sure also that she wants change or this wish list may scare her off. This is a risky move, but the rewards can be great.

To format a credible wish list you must lead off with what you are willing to do before you ask for what you want. Here's a typical wish list.

- ◆ My department will take full responsibility for updating the employee handbooks if we can lease a copier that collates.
- ◆ My staff will increase the number of seminars they conduct for internal employees by 12 percent if I am allowed to institute flextime.
- ◆ My staff will reduce paper costs by 6 percent if at year end they can take one third of the savings to purchase new office furniture and desk top items for their offices. Morale should improve since their offices have deteriorated badly since they moved in ten years ago.

◆ I can reduce the end-of-year problems related to closing out the budget by hiring a temp for eight days. Although I don't yet know the specific numbers, there should be a savings because fewer mistakes will be made if the employees aren't here so late, night after night. This solution might also help with the recent turnover problem. (Be realistic. Limit the number of days you request for temps. Be specific.)

Before you take the risk of asking the boss to spend this money, you might want to run it past someone who works for her.

3. Ask for an orientation, perhaps conducted by a coworker, and a written job description. Go over the job description with your new boss before signing the contract. Better employers will want to do this. They will respect you for wanting to be prepared.

4. Ask your boss how she prefers to be communicated with about both daily issues and more important tactical issues. What works best for her? E-mail? Scheduled meetings? Casual conversations? Lunch? Early morning? Five o'clock? Include a statement like the following:
   You have given me a lot of insight into this job that will be helpful. I'd like to feel that you could give me similar help if I ever run into a tactical problem a week or a month from now. I know you're busy. If we needed to talk, what would work best for you as far as time and place?

5. Make the top of your desk look neat and clean. Even if you have to hide a box of stuff in your car until tomorrow, get your desk in immaculate shape on Day One. It may not be logical, but many people form a view of your professionalism and organizational skills from appearances. Look organized.

6. Smile, smile, smile. If you don't,

   ◆ some people will think you look sneaky and distrust you.
   ◆ some people will think you look hostile and be hostile in return.
   ◆ some people will think you look shy and run all over you.
   ◆ some people will think you look confused and dumb (and tell everyone in the company).

7. Write a one-paragraph article for the company newsletter. Entitle it, "An Outsider's View." Cite all the pleasant surprises you have had so far. Thank the individuals who helped you if there is enough space.

8. Define a routine that will make you more productive than you were in your last job. You know the times of day that potentially can rob you of optimum productivity. You may take three cups of coffee to get started in the morning or you may lose focus or get chatty in midafternoon. Build a schedule that takes your predilections into account.

   A lot of silent contracting goes on during the first week at work. Give your coworkers cues that your productive time is morning or afternoon. Be friendly and encouraging as they welcome you.

Keep watch for people who want to come by and chat every afternoon.

9. The following is the ideal for your first week. Your schedule may not allow it. This is only a guide.

◆ Go to each of your coworkers privately and tell each you're happy to work with him. You may have had a brief introduction earlier, but this is your chance to be Mohammed going to the mountain. As far as etiquette goes, they should be coming to you to welcome you. Your reaching out to them will be disarming. This is a gesture showing that you want to become an integral, supportive member of the group.

◆ On your fourth day, leave handwritten notes to the one or two people who helped you most. Thank them. Mention specific things they did that were helpful.

◆ Turn something in. Deliver something to your boss. Finish something your first week. If you can't think of anything useful to do, write up one of the following:

– Summarize what you learned and observed during Week One. Itemize what you plan to do next week. Run it by a coworker for input.

– Create a folder called "New Employee Orientation." Insert helpful brochures, bits of information, and a list of suggestions that should be done next time. Do not criticize anyone for things not done this time. Just give it to your boss to use with the next new employee.

– Make a list with two headings: *Tasks* and *Contributions*. Under tasks, put everything you did this week. Under contributions, write what positive results came out of these tasks. This list should also give credit to other people for the contributions they've made.

◆ Arrive early every day and stay a little late. Some internal company critics are clock-watchers. Don't blow it your first week. They won't be watching as closely as time goes on and you prove yourself.

10. Have you taken a job that someone else wanted? You should ask this question before beginning any job. Don't ignore that. Find out a little about the person who was passed over. Go to her during your first few days. Include the following in your conversation.

◆ acknowledgment of special skills and abilities she has
◆ empathy
◆ ask for help

The conversation might go something like this:

Angela, I know that you are the manager with the most experience, the best managerial skills, and the best candidate for my job from inside the company. All I can figure out is that they wanted someone from the outside for some reason. If I were in your position, I'd be very disappointed. That's happened to me before so I don't blame you if you feel that way, but I've come to ask for your help. I hope you won't hold my getting this job against me, because I need your expertise if I'm going to succeed.

Note: Do not ever say that she is the better candidate or put yourself down.

What do you do if you have become the manager of your peers? This is doubly complicated when, as above, you have been chosen over people you must work with every day! So what do you do if suddenly your coworkers have to call you boss?

You need a defining moment when your identity officially changes. Often, word simply circulates that you have gotten the promotion, but there is no official acknowledgment. If you are changing from a peer to a superior, you need a public moment to assume your new identity. Even if your boss has named you to this position in a staff meeting, you still need to have your own meeting or event in which you publicly take the helm.

For most people, the best time to do this is at the first staff meeting you hold. Other kickoff events could be

◆ a team-building session with a professional consultant
◆ a sales incentive or motivational meeting

Your First Staff Meeting

Although it is usually unwise to go in making sweeping changes the first week, in your first meeting you should announce one or two changes if you are in management to show that you have taken charge. In your first meeting the following events should occur.

1. Announce one or two uncontroversial changes you will be making. These should be changes that you know you can implement smoothly. You don't want your first bold move to backfire on you. Choose changes that ensure you will get cooperation from the whole staff. Try to implement a popular change, one that people have been wanting for some time. Bring this change up in a confident, but not dictatorial or threatening way. Don't be critical of how things worked in the past. Say something like: "Like many of you, I've seen things I'd like to do around here if I ever had the opportunity. One thing I'd like to do is . . ."

2. Do something to ask for input about how things should be done going forward. You don't want to be a dictator. Following the changes you just announced by asking for input makes you look less threatening. Consider asking for input in one of these ways:

- ◆ a brief survey
- ◆ a suggestion box
- ◆ a scheduled meeting for brainstorming and idea generation
- ◆ a three-item wish list from each person

Have them complete these sentences:
If I were manager, I would immediately _____ .
If I were manager, by year-end I would _____ .

3. Talk a little about a system(s) or project(s) that is working well and vow to support that. Underscore that many things will not change.
4. End with expectations and encouragement.
   I look forward to serving as Marketing Director. You know me; I like to work hard and I believe in teamwork. My expectations are pretty much what you'd expect from me. They include the following:

- ◆ Give it all you've got on the job.
- ◆ Take care of yourselves to achieve balance between work and your life after five.
- ◆ Communicate early and often if a problem arises so I can support you fully.

Thank you.

The second-worst thing you can do is act like a wimp during this critical take-charge period. That will make many things you'll have to do in the months to come harder.

The very *worst* thing you can do is to be perceived as a power-mad dictator who has forgotten from whence he came. Take charge, but take care to show respect and appreciation to the people who can make or break you in this position.

The Politically Wise Way to Exit a Job

You may have left your job because another company will pay more. You may have left because you can't stand your boss or the department or some coworkers. For whatever reason you are leaving, you should leave on a positive note. Why?

1. You may need a reference in five weeks or five years. Things can change. Unfortunately, you have a link to this place forever because it will always be part of your work history.
2. Even if your official reference is good, coworkers and bosses can hurt your future career moves with a tone or a hint if a new employer calls—even years later! Make sure you leave friends behind, not enemies, even if you have to eat a little crow.
3. A coworker or manager in your old company may take a high-level position at a growing new company. He may be in the position to hire you for your dream job. Be sure he remembers you only as a professional, a pleasure to work with. Don't carry baggage.
4. Believe it or not, years later you may go back. People who thought they couldn't get out of a company fast enough are amazed to find themselves going back years later. A few of the reasons people are pleased to return to a company they once left include the following:

   ◆ They are hired back at a higher level and can have more control to effect changes.
   ◆ They left to take a better job but the realities of increased travel or lack of retirement benefits or other lifestyle issues caused them to have a new appreciation for the old company.

Getting married or having children can also alter one's viewpoint.

◆ The old company goes through a merger or other management change that makes it a better fit philosophically.

◆ The employee's new company goes through a similar change that makes it unattractive.

◆ The employee is the last one hired and first one fired when the new company downsizes or merges. With the job market flooded in his field, he returns to the familiar old company.

◆ Your old company merges with your new one!

For these and many other reasons, always leave a job in such a way that people would be pleased to see you come back.

Strategic Moves for Leaving a Job

1. Even if it's brief, leave a basic orientation sheet for the person who inherits your job. List what must be done and on what days/times. Give names and phone numbers of people who can serve as resources for each task. Give any little tips you've learned along the way. All organizations have quirks. Don't make the new guy learn the hard way.

   List hot items for Week One as well as long-term goals. Leave samples of forms, correctly filled out, and other helpful job aids. In your last couple of weeks on the job, make a point to make a copy of most everything you do to save as an example. Put all this in a nice-looking folder and give it to your boss to be sure you get credit.

   Also, you may be asked to train your replacement. Be very kind and complimentary to this person; she may be running this department in five years and will be asked to give you a reference or verify your job history.

2. Chat one on one with each person you work with during your last week. Tell each what you value in him, such as

◆ what he models
◆ what he has taught you
◆ what area of his strength you wish you had
◆ an accomplishment he had while you've known him
◆ what contribution you think he will make in the future

This will be easy with your friends but if you have had conflict with a coworker, you should consider doing this anyway. Some of the best referrals and references will come from people who initially have given you a really hard time. There is a bond some people feel with you if you have had a rough patch and worked through it. Even if you don't have a warm relationship, they may respect you and want to end on a positive note. Usually, you can find one thing to respect or admire in even the least likeable person, so consider telling difficult coworkers what you value in them also.

3. Attempt to always leave a job for a better opportunity—at least for the record. When you resign you will be asked to fill out forms and write a letter of resignation stating why you are leaving. You may even have an exit interview. In addition to these official opportunities to state your reasons, unofficially many people will be asking, "Why?"

Be selective about what you say. You may be leaving to diversify your experience, but mainly because you hate your boss. Choose to dwell on the positive reasons: to diversify your experience. It's a much better reflection on you to omit that you don't see eye to eye with the boss. To the extent that you ethically can do this, leave out personal reasons for leaving such as relationship problems and failure to receive recognition.

It's also not a good idea to list other personal reasons for leaving such as to spend more time with your children or to care for an elderly person. Unfortunately, these reasons could hurt your marketability the next time you enter the job market. Despite what the buzz is from enlightened corporations, most companies want you to abstain from having any personal problems. For the record, you can be that person with no personal problems.

Here are some great answers to list as your official reasons for leaving a job.

◆ You want to explore doing some things on the Internet because you think that's where the future of your industry is.

◆ You believe you need to gain more experience in

    _____ .

◆ You need to get some diversity in your background.

◆ You're young and it's a great time to make a change.

◆ You've been with this company a long time, and if you're ever going to try something new, now is the time.

◆ You've been offered a fascinating (great, valuable) new job.

◆ You're going into business for yourself.

Sample Letter of Resignation

When you resign, submit an official letter of resignation.

Dear Mr. Brownlow:

Despite the great regard I have for Baker International and the management, I submit my resignation, effective June 30, 2008.

In the five years that I have worked with Baker International, I have watched the company grow from a 50 million dollar company to a 150 million dollar company. Thank you for all the wonderful opportunities these last five years have afforded me.

Thanks to Bob Faulkner, my manager, and the leadership of Ellen Manville, Vice President of Operations, I have developed professionally and personally.

I will be leaving to assume the position of Director of Sales for ATCO Services.

With continued respect,

Jill Brown

---

4. Write a note thanking the Human Resources people for the professional way they handled your exodus. In fact, at the beginning of this process you should visit the HR person who will be handling your termination. Offer to help in any way to facilitate the process. Tell him you need his expert assistance in leaving in a professional manner and will appreciate any advice.

    The Human Resources Department will often handle any queries from future employers about your job performance and stability. Make sure your next boss hears a smile in the voice of the Human Resources rep when your name is mentioned.

5. Be sure to carry with you any benefits due you when you leave. Ask the Human Resources rep to tell you what you can take with you. If you are leaving to be self-employed, you most probably need to take the health insurance with you. You can usually do this for 18 months, at your own expense, of course.

6. Write letters to the executives of your division thanking them for the opportunities they gave you while you were there. Cite what you have learned. Mention any personal favors or cite any quotes of theirs. Cite specifically and wish them luck on their upcoming initiatives.

7. Leave everything uncluttered, organized, and very clean. No matter how high up you go, you usually have to do the final cleanup yourself—and I do mean with a strong spray cleaner. This is your final stamp of professionalism.

8. Write one or two letters of commendation or thanks for coworkers or staff. Ask that these letters be placed in their personnel files. This is the best departing gift you can give someone. These people may be in a position to hire you one day—even at another company.

9. Write two unsolicited letters of recommendation before you leave. If you know that your secretary has wanted to become

the department's travel coordinator for a long time, write a letter recommending him for that role before you leave. Even if the position is not currently open, the letter can go on file. Also, give the secretary a copy so he can use it the next time the job opens up.

Or, if someone who served on a focus group with you is the Manager of Residential Sales and aspires to be Vice President of Sales, write a letter before you leave telling upper management what a fine job she has done in the group. Point out how these qualities would make her a great vice president—qualities such as

◆ creative solutions
◆ good follow-up skills
◆ well organized
◆ leadership
◆ innovative and open to ideas of others
◆ high energy; dynamic

You never know. Leaving behind these legacies may pay off in unexpected ways. These people may be in influential positions later when you are in the job market again. Their gratitude for your gesture may prompt them to go to bat for you.

10. Purge files of any personal or unpleasant correspondence that you legally can remove. Documents live on.

ACTION ITEMS

If you are about to leave your job do A.
If you are not about to resign do B.

A. Do three of the activities from this chapter in the next week.

Suggestions:

1. Write a positive letter of resignation.

2. Meet with coworkers.

3. Create orientation file for new employee.

B. Think back to the last job from which you resigned. Also, reconsider the first months of your current job. List any steps in this chapter that would have been helpful or strategic. Which would have helped you build better relationships faster?

1. _____

2. _____

3. _____

Chapter 9

◆

How to Handle Your Coworkers and Staff So They Will Make You a Star

Never lose sight of the fact that the most important yardstick of your success will be how you treat other people—your family, friends, and coworkers, and even strangers you meet along the way.

—Barbara Bush

What's the strategy for making your staff and coworkers want to make you look good? It's not to dazzle them with your brilliance or credentials. It's not to outwork them with long hours. And it's not empty flattery and lots of rah-rah speeches. Those don't get you much mileage over the long term.

Actually, the basic strategy is simple. It boils down to trust.

TRUST: THE SECRET WEAPON FOR INFLUENCING OTHERS

If your coworkers and staff see that you are very real, very authentic in what you say and how you respond to them, they're going to be a lot more accepting of your little flaws and idiosyncrasies. They can relax in your presence, and that makes working with you a pleasure.

Building trust, however, is a process that requires that you demonstrate your trustworthiness rather than hype it.

A DOZEN CARDINAL RULES FOR SUCCESS WITH COWORKERS AND STAFF

1. Whatever you do, don't lie, exaggerate, fudge, or mislead in any way. Peers and staff are unforgiving about this. The best possible strategy is to be candid and straightforward. We all know, however, there are times we just can't tell the unvarnished truth. In those situations (which should be few and far between), it is perfectly acceptable to punt. Here are some punting strategies.

   ◆ Defer or postpone. Say, "I'll get back to you."
   ◆ Pass the buck. Say, "That's really Jim's area of expertise."
   ◆ Avoid the situation/person.
   ◆ Answer a question with a question. Say, "What have been the problems leading up to this?"
   ◆ Answer most of the question, but avoid tricky parts.
   ◆ Reiterate and redefine the options. Give the problem back to the other person and ask him to choose the right answer.

2. Do what you say you'll do. Follow through. If you say you'll get back to someone, do so in a timely manner. If you say you'll provide information to someone, get it to her sooner rather than later.

   One success story I have followed in recent years has been John Woodley. Woodley excelled as a manager for energy giant Southern Company, later becoming something of a resident futurist and visionary for them. Although he had his challenges in the corporate politics of this conservative legacy company, he was absolutely adored by his staff and coworkers, despite his eccentricities. In an interview for this book, he said his credo was, "Underpromise, overdeliver." Apparently, he delivered handsomely. When Morgan Stanley decided to establish trading in energy futures, they wooed this talented young man away with a dream job, an exponential increase in compensation, and future career opportunities that few of his peers could ever imagine. His strategy may not sound exciting but it works.

3. Be consistent. Don't consistently push your staff to rush to produce, take risks, and meet deadlines at any cost and then beat them up if there is a careless error in the rush. Conversely, if you pressure them to dot every *i* and cross every *t*, don't suddenly come down on them for not rushing a job.

   People get used to your style. If you abruptly change styles, they are thrown off balance. They may think you are unstable, dishonest, or unreasonable.

   Of course, there are times that everyone needs to alter style to meet a deadline or successfully complete a project. If you do need to switch styles, communicate that to your coworkers or staff. Say, "I know that I usually preach meeting the deadline no matter what it takes. Meeting the deadline on this project is important, too, but accuracy is even more critical this time. Please double-check everything, even if it takes a bit more time. Come see me if you see that the extra precautions may cause you to miss the deadline. Maybe I can help you."

   Communicating your temporary switch in philosophy will put to rest any rumors that you're a schizophrenic tyrant who is impossible to please.

4. Keep all staff and coworkers in your communication loop. Nothing makes the people you work with more paranoid than being left out of your communication loop.

   If you are contemplating a change, either tell no one or update everyone you work with, at least partially, so that no one feels left out.

5. Talk about people behind their backs—in a good way. Nothing gets you in solid with people like having them hear that you built them up to someone else behind their backs. Good gossip often gets back to the person you support. The response is extremely beneficial to you.

    ◆ Your coworker trusts you more than ever.
    ◆ Good gossip is often reciprocated.
    ◆ You are viewed by others in the organization as a team player instead of a backstabber. That makes people want to promote you or steal you away.
    ◆ You reflect some of that success when you talk about the success of a coworker or staff member. Just as there is guilt by association, there is success by association.

6. Be here now. Though highly controversial, pop psychology guru Werner Erhard changed thousands of lives by espousing the philosophy of living totally in the here and now. He had some good points. People who operate out of what's going on today rather than yesterday or the murkiness of tomorrow have these advantages.

    ◆ Taking people at face value rather than typecasting them because of their past experiences and roles opens you up to new possibilities. Learn to use resources more creatively. Although I do believe some thought should be given to past performance and long-term consequences, the bulk of our energy should be invested in today.
    ◆ People are more productive on today's projects when they're not anxious over what may happen in the future.
    ◆ Grudges or bad feelings from the past don't hinder their having a good working relationship with someone today.

7. Don't waste anyone's time. Everyone is so pressed for time today that wasting a coworker's or staff member's valuable time can send her straight over the edge. Don't make the mistake of being inconsiderate of other people's time. Here are the basics.

◆ Always be on time for meetings/appointments. You actually have to be a little early to ensure you're on time. Nothing tells a staff member that you don't value what they do more than keeping him (or a roomful of them), sitting there waiting for you.

◆ Don't make a habit of canceling meetings, changing your mind, requesting information then not using it, or causing rework.

◆ Don't schedule meetings, training, or anything unless you have explored whether it's a good use of employee time. Check it out. Get references. Do some groundwork. If one of your experienced sales reps has to miss a day of commissions while he attends a very basic seminar on selling by a less experienced instructor, he is going to lose respect for you if you have required him to attend.

◆ Keep work phone calls and conversations brief—less than five minutes.

8. Observe the little everyday courtesies that make worklife pleasant. In our fast-paced, high-pressure work environment, we sometimes let "please" and "thank you" slide—when the secretary gives you your messages, your coworker reminds you of something, your assistant furnishes you with information. Yes, they're just doing their jobs, but the "please" and "thank you" just oil the mechanism of a finely tuned organization.

9. Be loyal. If someone inside or outside your department disparages a coworker or staff member, don't join in the beat 'em up

session. You may not want to offend the complainer, but you can at least take the neutral position. Consider these responses:

Have you addressed these problems with her? I know she'd want to change things if she realized . . .

He probably hasn't seen it in that light. Would you mind if I brought it to his attention?

That's a shame. She's usually so attentive. I wonder what the problem was.

Would you like me to look into it?

I can't imagine what happened. I really think you two should talk. You'll find he's very professional about taking constructive criticism.

10. Develop the art of putting yourself in the other person's place. No book can spell out how to handle every situation. We all have multiple priorities, and choosing the right thing to do can be complex. Learn to use your imagination to "become the other person" for a moment. How would he view your behavior? What would he expect you to do? What would he consider the right or ethical thing to do? What does he have at stake? What would be his hopes in the situation? Factor all that in before you make an impetuous decision that could cost you a valued ally.

11. Share freely and considerately. This doesn't just pertain to office supplies, food, and credit. Many opportunities for sharing equitably arise daily.

Time off

Vacation scheduling can easily cause rifts among a team of coworkers. Be considerate of your teammates. Don't always get in there first and take the prime days/weeks off just because you were able to beat the others to the punch. If possible, discuss your days requested and see if they work for others.

Volunteer to work your share of holiday time or weekend days. And if you're dealing with staff, be willing to work some of the same holidays they do. Model what you ask them to do.

Sharing credit

For every project, for every award, for every good sales year, usually there is one person acknowledged as a star. If you are the star, give credit away to others. That only makes you look like more of a star.

At work, use the word "we" instead of "I" when asked how you accomplished things. Include your teammates in any recognition or compliments. They will return the favor.

12. Learn to work out problems and conflict in an amicable, win/win way. Even if we like our coworkers and staff, problems will arise. Develop a very solution-oriented, problem-solving approach as soon as differences arise.

    Never bring up a problem unless you have a suggestion for a solution or even several options. Your coworker may not like your solution, but now the burden is on her to develop a solution if she rejects yours.

When you bring up a problem, follow these guidelines.

- Begin the conversation by saying what you value about the coworker.
- Acknowledge that you agree on most/many things and that this is just an isolated problem.
- Stay focused on the issue and don't comment on personalities or motives. Don't stray to past problems or other issues.
- Suggest a solution. Better yet, offer your coworker several options.
- If the coworker accepts your solution, your problem is solved. If not, ask him to get back to you with a solution that works for him. Ask him to choose a time for the two of you to meet to explore his suggestions. Try to get a commitment for a meeting.
- End by thanking him for his time and for working things out with you.

Whatever you do, don't let this escalate into a bitter or loud argument. That reflects badly on you. Even if your coworker loses his temper, don't react the same way. By keeping control, you will display power and leadership—a long-term gain.

You never know how making an enemy now can hurt you in the future—even after you have left this company. The person you anger now may handle the phone call verifying your employment and checking references for a job you apply for five years from now. Leave on good terms.

DON'T REPEAT THE SAME MISTAKES

What really bugs some people is when you make the same mistake a second or third time. People who forgive easily the first time may not do so if you don't take care to prevent the same thing from happening again. Learn from your mistakes.

Review the methods of handling bosses in Chapters 3 and 4. Many of these strategies apply to coworkers.

Note: The Dozen Cardinal Rules above are the biggies. To thrive daily among your staff and coworkers, these are the foundation. If you are faithful in these things, people will be more forgiving of your mistakes. More important, they will be generous in their backing of you as you strive to move ahead. In today's companies, you need the support of others to succeed for the long term. You may see some short-term success for people who violate one or more of these rules, but the consequences will eventually catch up with them.

ACTION ITEMS

1. List below the two coworkers who are your strongest allies.

   A. _____

   B. _____

   List below the two coworkers who are not strongly supportive of you or even adversarial.

   C. _____

   D. _____

2. Review the Cardinal Rules in this chapter. Which of the Cardinal Rules do you need to pay special attention to with each coworker above? Have you violated any of the rules with one of these coworkers? What can you do to demonstrate that you are observing the Cardinal Rules with each person above? Write a brief summary of what you will do over the next six weeks to demonstrate that you are adhering to the Cardinal Rules with each coworker.

   Coworker A: _____

   Coworker B: _____

   Coworker C: _____

   Coworker D: _____

Chapter 10

Answers to Frequently Asked Questions: The Dirty Dozen

Life is like high school, it's small and everybody talks about everybody.

—AP, January 5, 2007

1. **A coworker of mine and I are beginning a romantic relationship. Do you have any advice?**

First, are you really sure you want to change the relationship from a professional or even friendly one to a romantic one? Office romances have much potential for harm to both participants and very little upside in most cases. Are there really no other persons you might just as easily date outside of work who would not harm your relationship with peers and management on your job? Often, two people who start an office romance think only of how their relationship with one another will be affected, but the romance can also alter the dynamics of your relationships with everyone else at work. One or both persons losing their jobs is not unheard of.

People used to believe that a basic rule of professionalism was to keep business and personal lives separate, meaning one should not date a coworker. We all know enough people who have met their spouses through work to know that this rule is just not practical. After all, we spend more of our time on the job than anywhere else we might meet a person with whom we have something in common. So if you have weighed the possibilities of damage to your career and to the friendships and you still intend to go for it, here are some guidelines:

◆ First, find out if there is a policy in your office about this type of fraternization and be sure you adhere to it.

◆ Second, the relationship must be initiated by the person who is in the subordinate position. For example, if your coworker is an administrative assistant and you are a manager, the administrative assistant must initiate the relationship; otherwise, the romance could be viewed as sexual harassment. As the relationship escalates, say from nonsexual to sexual, the subordinate must always be the person to make the next move.

◆ Remove yourselves from decision-making that could be viewed as biased by colleagues. For example, if you are to determine bonuses for a group that includes a person you are involved with, you need to find someone else to evaluate that person or change to a committee or survey-based means of awarding bonuses. One of the most unfair things that happens in a relationship in which a boss determines pay or career advances is that the subordinate's track record of hard work and achievement becomes overshadowed by comments such as, "Well, he was dating the boss so he was bound to get that promotion (raise, etc.)."

◆ Public displays of affection are considered in bad taste but displays between coworkers are even worse, earning the disrespect of colleagues whose support you may one day need to be successful in your job.

◆ Have a plan for ending the relationship. Right now, you may not be able to imagine ending the relationship, but the reality is that most relationships do end eventually. Talk *now* about how you will handle the breakup with each other and colleagues when the relationship does end: How will you communicate this to others? Will you continue to work closely with each other or will one of you transfer? What about mutual friends at work? Who will lunch with whom?

2. **One of my peers at work is having a romantic relationship with our boss. I am aware of it though they think no one knows. She is constantly being shown favor and given prime assignments due to his favor toward her. What should I do?**

    In your career, you will have to endure some things that are just patently unfair and this is probably one of them. First, you would have to have solid evidence of an affair if you were to take action, and that is usually impractical unless you have the money to hire a detective (over-the-top) to document the relationship. If you are thinking of complaining to someone above the boss's head, you can't speak a word with only observations and circumstantial evidence. Also, there is a very good chance that your management already knows all about the affair and either does not care or may be taking a cautious approach and not taking action in the hopes it will end soon. Take a cue and realize that most companies operate on a don't-ask-don't-tell basis on office romances and usually don't appreciate anyone making an issue of it.

    And even if you are right and your accusations are taken seriously, most teams don't like a whistleblower. I am not saying that there is never a time to take action in an unfair situation like this, but you should realize that the potential risk to your relationship with others (not just the lovers but your entire department) is great.

    In most cases, not saying anything but documenting your own contributions and making sure your boss knows of your value is a faster way to being rewarded with prime assignments. If you show your resentment toward your boss or peer, he or she will be even more allied against you. If you really find the situation unbearable, you may take the risk of going to your boss to discuss how to get what you want. This talk should never mention his interest in your peer; it should be purely professional. Say something like: "I am interested in handling more industrial assignments in addition to commercial. I feel I have proven that I am capable of succeeding in these assignments based on (show the successes you have been documenting). Would you lay out for me what I need to do to be assigned the next industrial client?"

Having the choice put to him this way may make the boss feel he needs to assign the next industrial job to you, based on your abilities and not because you threatened anything.

There is a time to go to an HR rep and talk about a long-term problem like this, but be sure you do not say anything you cannot prove. If you do, you may be looking at a slander suit against you. And even if you win, the negative gossip and fallout may follow you in this job and onto the next. Sometimes it means less stress and loss to you to simply transfer out of the department and find a less dysfunctional group. After several other people transfer, your management will realize that something is wrong even if no one blows the whistle.

3. **I am being sexually harassed by my boss. It started as just suggestive talk but has recently evolved into some very uncomfortable closed-door sessions in his office. The tension is terrible as I need to keep my job, but I am in a committed relationship and do not want this type of attention. What should I do?**

Even if you were not in a committed relationship, you should not have to hear one sexually suggestive word from a boss, much less be subjected to these closed-door sessions. You may have already done these things, but here are the basics:

◆ Never reinforce inappropriate behavior by paying any attention to it initially. We often laugh at sexual innuendo because it makes us uncomfortable; with a sexual predator, that is a mistake. He takes that as the green light for more sexually explicit behavior. When you hear a sexual remark at work, busy yourself elsewhere, walk out of the room, go to your computer, and withdraw all interest in the conversation.

◆ Be sure that your clothes and demeanor are professional and not provocative.

◆ If pressed for a reaction or if told you are a prude or worse, simply say that you have too much to do to participate in those conversations at work and that you would appreciate not being included in the future. Keep it brief, don't lecture and don't sound morally superior.

◆ Does your company have an Employee Assistance Program that will keep what you say confidential? Even if you are being harassed, you may suffer if you take action against a popular or powerful manager. Be sure that before you tell anyone, you are ready for a backlash effect that will make you feel even more victimized than you already are. There are times to speak up, especially if you are not the first victim of this person. Still, be aware that you may suffer more consequences than the perpetrator.

◆ You must insist on all meetings being open door or attended by a third person, even if you risk losing your job. You may feel that you will never get as good a job as this one, but that may not be true. Start looking now so that you will not be in a trap when you give this predator an ultimatum.

4. **I have two colleagues who have been in a feud for over six months. We all used to be friends, so both know that I speak to the other. They are always asking me what the other person**

said about things or what they are doing. Also, each is disappointed in me for remaining friends with the other. What should I do?

Tell each colleague that the only things you are going to tell the other person is what is public knowledge. Let's say the two colleagues are Brett and John. If Brett makes a statement in a meeting with two peers, you can repeat that conversation since it is company common knowledge.

Also, ask the colleagues not to put you in the middle any longer by asking questions.

Finally, be clear in your own mind that this is not your problem to fix. If either comes to you to ask you to advocate or mediate, be ready with the name of a great counselor or HR person for them to see. Recommend that both colleagues go together and leave you out of the process.

And be careful. I have often seen the friend who tries to be the go-between wind up being the person whom neither party remained friends with even after a feud is patched up. Just say No to all attempts to draw you into taking sides, even when the lure is cleverly disguised as asking you to be helpful and concerned.

5. There are seven administrative assistants in my company. Some have very busy offices and some have so little to do that they get bored. My office has twice as much of a workload as most of the offices. I do not mind working hard but my workload has grown to the point that it is impossible to get everything done. What should I do?

Numbers speak to executives and strategic planners who make the decisions on workload issues and hiring. Have you tracked each component of your workload? Number of phone calls? Number of visitors? Pages typed? Projects handled? Armed with this information, you can approach a sympathetic executive and ask if similar studies have been done in other offices. If so, you can compare your numbers and prove your point. If not, you are armed and ready for the administration to do its own assessment and arrive at the same conclusion you have.

Also, be ready with a suggestion. Most companies do not want to hire extra help, so consider if a shared receptionist with another area is a partial solution to diminishing your workload. Having this kind of support ready along with a solution and not just a complaint increases your chances of getting some relief.

If this does not work, begin to find out if you can transfer to a department that has a lighter workload. If you have an outstanding reputation as a worker in your company, you can say to your manager, "Doing excellent work is important to me. I really love our work in this department but with the increased workload I don't think I can continue to guarantee that everything will be done with the excellence I desire. I probably need to go to a different department where I can complete everything on time and with the care I want to give it. With a 20 percent increase in the number of phone calls and the 15 percent increase in appointments this year, there simply are not enough hours in the day to do all things well in this department." This is a high-risk approach, so only use it if you are ready to move on and know you have a job waiting.

6. **I had some family problems last year and know that I am gossiped about quite a bit at work. How should I handle this?**

    Ignoring gossip is the best way for it to die a natural death. There will be someone else with a new tidbit in their lives that will be the focus for these folks eventually.

Some gossips are immature and if you act as if they aroused a defensive response from you, they will enjoy torturing you with their gossip far longer than if they had seen no response from you.

And don't let the gossip make you self-conscious. Be friendly and outgoing. Some people act so self-conscious that they perpetuate the gossip longer. If you are unfriendly and aloof because you feel people are talking about you, it will make them talk more.

7. **I work in a traditional corporation of around 10,000 employees. One look at the executive boardroom or any high-level managerial meeting will tell you that the good ol' boy network is alive and well as they promote their own. I have risen to a higher-level management position than most women, but the ol' boy system bugs me. What can I do?**

    ◆ If you can't beat them, join them. Guys become supporters of one another usually through things they do. Be sure you are volunteering to work for these guys on races, marathons, fundraisers, and other causes that they are involved in. And learn golf or tennis or other activities that the ol' boys are participating in. Do be careful, however, not to cross the line and go where you will be resented. For example, if there is a hunting trip for the guys and accommodations for you will be a problem, you might want to consider foregoing this trip and not make them uncomfortable. Use common sense. You don't need to stick up for your rights every time and become a foe in the process.
    ◆ Be sure you are doing for the women at the level below you what you wished had been done for you. Mentor and advocate for the women you can help. It will come back to you.
    ◆ Seek out mentors and peer coaches to sponsor you. Don't be discouraged if the first people you approach are not generous

or helpful. Keep trying. Eventually, you will build your own good ol' girl network.

8. **I am working with a great guy who has impeccable integrity and work habits. He is just not very good at his job. His lack of expertise affects the performance of our team. I like him but I feel something must be done so that our work product and my career goals won't be affected. What should I do?**

   ◆ Have you asked your coworker what attracted him to this job in the first place? Perhaps he is as uncomfortable in this role as you are in having him in the role. If he opens up and talks about not feeling he has the skills needed, then be ready with suggestions about openings you know of in other departments or companies.

   ◆ Have you tried to realign duties so that he will be doing parts of the job that he is best at and avoids the areas that will affect your performance most? Often in your career you will need to "shadow manage" one of your peers by reorganizing tasks and duties so that everyone's best gifts are applied productively.

   ◆ Is it time for you to move on? Sometimes managers and coworkers depend on us to fix things instead of fixing the problems themselves. If you were to go to a different department, would this person perhaps improve out of necessity or get training?

   ◆ Ask your boss to implement a peer coaching program. Be sure someone else is assigned to coach your less competent peer. Perhaps someone else will mention the problem to your boss.

9. **I work in a family-owned company and I am not part of the family. At times, I cannot be as direct about problems that have occurred because the problem was created by a family member. Any advice?**

◆ You clearly have already realized the first rule: These are family members first and employees second. Any rational approach will have to be tempered by the reality that there is an irrational element in family relationships that you will never completely be able to disregard. You are wise to proceed cautiously.

◆ A pride of ownership of a business gives most families a sense of entitlement to be more forgiving to family members and to be more generous with money and promotions. Even if you have never seen that come into play, you may see it more as older members start retiring. Although some heirs do not want to run the family business and are content to let others do so, you may never reach the position you want if all family members decide to stay active in the business.

◆ There are some excellent consulting firms that specialize in family businesses. If you can tactfully suggest that one of these firms help with a non-family issue, perhaps a consultant can address the nepotism problem while they are there.

◆ Consider asking for a session on career planning with someone qualified to know the future direction of the company. Ask candidly what the company's five-year plan is for you. If there is not a great deal of opportunity for you, it is better to know now. This is one of those risky steps that should be taken only if you are prepared to look outside the company for your next position.

10. **The morale in our company is not good. It is not that it is so negative but that people just have no initiative or desire to make the business better and more profitable. I see other companies that are doing much better than we are in this economy. Can anything be done about attitude or culture?**

◆ There are great tools for surveying and defining problems in a corporate culture. Often by identifying exactly what the problems are through a corporate climate survey or culture assessment, the leadership can focus on just the few things that need to be improved.

◆ Communication is usually one of the roots of a corporate culture weakness. Every company should have a company-wide communication plan from the top down.

◆ Study other companies similar to yours in size, industry, and other characteristics. What are their best practices? What can you adapt from them? What can you learn about them from Hoover's, a supplier of fact sheets and company profiles, or from research on the web or from their press?

◆ What can you do to institute more focus groups and other opportunities for cross-company communication?

11. **Last year, I made a mistake that cost our mid-size company quite a bit of money. A shift in the economy made what had looked like a good decision actually turn out to be a bad decision. How should I handle it?**

◆ Successful companies such as Coke and GE are concerned when they have managers who have never made a mistake; these cautious managers are not taking risks that are needed to take the company forward. The fact that you are still employed says that the company believes in you and is seeing the mistake as a blip on the screen and not a prediction of the future. Don't make a bigger deal of it by bringing it up yourself or continuing to apologize. Move on. If asked about it, always begin by saying that it was a learning experience you wish had not happened, but since it did that it taught you more than you could ever have learned in a graduate program on that subject. Say that you came out of it better qualified to make similar decisions in the future and you are looking forward to earning the confidence the company has shown in you.

◆ Are there economic programs or predictors you can put in place to aid you in staving off similar situations in the future?

◆ For awhile, when you offer new ideas, be sure you have research and expert backing when you make your presentation in order to increase the comfort level of those few doubters who may still be among the decision-makers. Help build their confidence in you.

12. **I have been asked to fudge numbers on a report to a regulatory agency. What should I do?**

◆ With thoughts of Enron I want to say, "Run!" Still, this type of pressure comes up often so you may want to stay and fight. First of all, determine if you are really being asked to fudge. If the company wants you to use a different but legitimate accounting method, that is one thing. Truly being asked to do something unethical is a different matter altogether, especially as jail terms are being handed out pretty frequently for behaviors that were once considered business-as-usual. I certainly would never allow a report that I had signed to be submitted if I did not agree with it. If you are asked to prepare a report, put the information that you believe to be true in the report. Offer to let the executive add or enhance it as he or she sees fit. Be sure that the person who is willing to take responsibility for the contents has his or her name on the cover sheet. Offer to provide the research or information the executive wants and tell the executive he or she can change the report if he or she wants to, based on the research.

- ◆ Another strategy is to play dumb. If you just continue not to understand what is wanted, sometimes the executives will find someone else to do the reporting. After all, they don't want to be too explicit.
- ◆ Look at the harm that could come from the false reporting. Do you have a moral or legal duty to be a whistleblower? It may end your career in an industry, but are the stakes so high that you cannot be silent?

Chapter 11

♦

Your Action Plans
for Success

Action is the antidote to despair.

—Joan Baez

Review the Action Items at the ends of Chapters 2 through 9.

On the following chart, list the five items that you believe are most critical to your success. Commit to completing these steps by a certain date.

Action Item	Specific Step(s) I Will Take	People and/or Resources I Will Need	Deadline
1.	1.	1.	1.
2.	2.	2.	2.
3.	3.	3.	3.
4.	4.	4.	4.
5.	5.	5.	5.

Your Signature _____
Signature of Your Mentor or Supervisor _____

After completing the chart, consider asking your mentor or boss to sign it. Agree to meet in 30 days to review your progress.

INDEX